HOTEL - MOTEL LAW

HOTEL - MOTEL LAW

A PRIMER ON INNKEEPER LIABILITY

By

J. GREGORY SERVICE, B.B.A., J.D.

Member, The Florida Bar
Department of Business Administration
Broward Community College
Pompano Beach, Florida

CHARLES C THOMAS • PUBLISHER

Springfield • Illinois • U.S.A.

Published and Distributed Throughout the World by

CHARLES C THOMAS • PUBLISHER
2600 South First Street
Springfield, Illinois 62717

ISBN 0-398-04883-5

Library of Congress Catalog Card Number: 83-5012

With THOMAS BOOKS *careful attention is given to all details of manufacturing and design. It is the Publisher's desire to present books that are satisfactory as to their physical qualities and artistic possibilities and appropriate for their particular use.* THOMAS BOOKS *will be true to those laws of quality that assure a good name and good will.*

Printed in the United States of America
Q-R-3

Library of Congress Cataloging in Publication Data

Service J. Gregory.
Hotel-motel law.

Includes index.
1. Hotels, taverns, etc. – Law and legislation – United States. I. Title.
KF951.S47 1983 343.73'07864794 83-5012
ISBN 0-398-04883-5 347.3037864794

For the Rose

PREFACE

THE lodging industry is today a major industry providing employment for hundreds of thousands of persons and is a vital part of the economy of many states. While frequently characterized by establishments representing huge capital investments and generating very large revenues, in many respects it also still resembles its earlier days. Currently there are many large corporations operating hundreds of units, but thousands of smaller, independently owned and operated hotels and motels also exist. Regardless of their size, more and more often hotels and motels are becoming involved in lawsuits, and this is today a common concern to all.

In this book it is the intent of the author to consider briefly the law in general and various bases of legal liability and then to examine some particular situations in which hotels and motels often find themselves involved in lawsuits. Becoming aware of potential problem areas should enable the innkeeper to take action to eliminate the problem or at least reduce the severity of it or the likelihood of it occurring. The book does not attempt to set up specific guidelines to be followed; that would be somewhat unrealistic. Rather, its purpose is to develop an awareness on the part of the reader of duties owed by innkeepers to their guests and potential liabilities faced by those operating hotels and motels if these duties are not met.

All issues and situations involving potential liability of a hotel or motel are not discussed herein, but the major, more frequently occurring problems are examined. While many actual cases are cited and court opinions quoted to illustrate various ideas, the text is written primarily in layman's terms. The book should be considered a useful tool for those interested in the area professionally, especially operating management. It should also prove useful to others concerned with liability aspects of the lodging industry. By becoming aware of certain problems and their possible consequences, the innkeeper should be better able to guide his or her actions effectively in a complex business environment.

CONTENTS

Page

Preface vii

Chapter

1. From Inn to Hotel 3
2. The Law and Legal System 13
3. Loss and Legal Liability 25
4. Loss of Guests' Property 32
5. Food Service Liability 47
6. Acts of Employees – Vicarious Liability 60
7. Acts of Third Persons 71
8. Security Personnel 81
9. Injuries Involving Physical Facilities 86
10. Miscellaneous Topics 95

Appendix A 101

Appendix B 103

Appendix C 107

Appendix D 109

Case Index 111

Subject Index 113

HOTEL - MOTEL LAW

CHAPTER 1

FROM INN TO HOTEL

THE United States of today is a society on the move. Demands of an ever more competitive business environment and the dynamics of our modern economy require an increasing number of businessmen and -women to travel in the course of their employment. Much of this travel is at least overnight, and a large percentage of it is now on an extended basis, frequently a distance from home. Partially as a result of this dramatic increase in travel there has developed a basic need for increased numbers of quality establishments providing food and lodging for these business travelers. The hospitality industry, and especially that portion of it encompassing hotels and motels, has expanded dramatically over the past few decades to serve this recognized need for temporary lodging. Large corporations, operating hundreds of units from coast to coast and providing thousands of rooms, as well as small individual owner-operated establishments are today a part of the dynamic and expanding hotel-motel industry.

While the business traveler has substantially contributed to growth of the industry, vacationers and pleasure travelers have also been a major factor in expansion. Over the years a generally expanding economy, rising disposable family incomes, additional time off from employment, and the basic desire to take a yearly vacation have resulted in increased family pleasure travel and thus contributed to the rising demand for temporary lodging accommodations. Even during those times of temporary economic downturn it appears that the average family makes a concerted effort still to take some time off and travel for a vacation during the course of the year.

The ultimate destination may be closer to home and the stay shorter, but typically the family vacation will be one of the last luxuries to be discontinued. Indeed, with many other families, the vacation of today is considered, if not a necessity, an earned entitlement, whereas in years past it was truly a luxury. The growth in recent years of the popularity of the "package tour" wherein transportation, food, and lodging are arranged in advance has encouraged increased vacation travel, as has the increase in the number of group tour offerings by various organizations and associations. Regardless of the means or motivation for this travel, it has meant increased lodging facilities being offered. An ever increasing number of foreign tourists are also visiting the United States yearly and have become very important to the tourist industry in states such as California and Florida, both frequent destinations for the domestic vacationer.

With increased travel it is also noteworthy that the basic nature of some lodging establishments has changed somewhat over time. Rather than being predominantly located in central urban areas, many hotels and motels have located near airports and the interstate highway system, enhancing their convenience to the traveling public. In addition to the lodging accommodations provided, various recreational facilities, from pools to tennis courts, are often available. Entertainment is a common feature of larger establishments, ranging from a piano bar to a plush gambling casino complex and showcase entertainment featuring star performers. In some instances rather than merely providing lodging the establishment is creating essentially a resort complex for the guest. Of course, lodging facilities on the grounds are common to many theme amusement parks, the lodging being an additional source of revenue.

Those persons and companies engaged in the hotel and motel industry today are faced with a potential host of legal problems. Some of these problems are shared in general with many other business operations, while others are unique to the hospitality industry itself with its close and continued contact with the public. This quasi-public nature of the business is one of the facets that distinguish this business endeavor from many others.

Lodging establishments in the modern business world are more and more often becoming involved in litigation arising from the conduct of their business. While many times lawsuits arising from an incident cannot entirely be prevented, an insight into potential problems and areas of legal liability should help the informed innkeeper to avoid some common trouble areas. The purpose of this book is to provide a basic introduction to the area of hotel and motel law. The author hopes that after reading it owners, managers, and employees of lodging establishments will be more aware of potential problem areas and take responsive action either to eliminate or reduce the risk posed by the situation. This book is not intended in any sense to be a "how to do it" discourse on avoiding suits. Rather, it is intended as an educational tool for use by those persons actively engaged in the industry. Forewarned is truly forearmed; often a degree of preventative action can avoid an unfortunate incident and lawsuit or at least act toward reducing liability.

An appropriate place to begin our inquiry into law relating to hotels and motels is perhaps to look back briefly at the history of the institutions, consider what they were, and examine how they have changed and evolved over the years. The roots of both trace back to the inns of prior years. Travelers, since the earliest of times, have sought places of temporary haven and rest on their journeys where they could obtain food and shelter. Often they found these through the hospitality of those persons living along their route of travel, a friendly farmer or rancher. Virtually since the earliest of times there have also been those enterprising individuals who made a business out of providing food and shelter for the weary traveler and his companions and servants, for a fee. Stable facilities and care for the travelers' horses were commonly provided as well.

An inn was a privately operated business establishment, but it also had a public character. It was a business that opened its doors to, and offered accommodations to, the public in general. It thus developed early in the common law that one who operated an inn did not have the privilege of picking and choosing his guests on an arbitrary basis. When operating this type of establishment for the benefit of and in service to the public the innkeeper became obligated to accommodate all fit and proper persons who applied to him for rooms, so long as he did in fact have accommodations available. If his available rooms were filled then he was generally within his rights to refuse potential guests, there normally being no obligation on his part to convert space not usually used for rooms to accommodate travelers. The innkeeper was privileged to refuse persons who were unfit, drunk, disorderly, or would pose danger to other guests, but he of course was obligated to be reasonable in making this determination; it did not provide a guise under which he could arbitrarily pick and choose. The liability of an innkeeper for wrongfully failing to accept a guest was early recognized in the English case of *Lane v. Cotten* [88 Eng. Rep. 1458 (K.B. 1701)] wherein the court stated:

> If an innkeeper refuse to entertain a guest where his house is not full, an action will lie against him. . . . If the inn be full, or the carriers' horses laden, the action would not lie for such refusal; but one that has made profession of a public employment, is bound to the utmost extent of that employment to serve the public.

The common law rule obligating an innkeeper to accept all fit and proper persons requesting accommodations, so long as they were available, became well established in the law of the United States as well. This rule, however, applied only to those persons who made a *business* of receiving guests. Occasionally the question would arise whether or not a person was in fact operating an inn so as to be subject to the rule. In an early case from Texas the court considered this question and the attendant liability of one who ran an inn. The court wrote in its opinion in *Howth v. Franklin* [20 Tex. 798 (1858)]:

> An innkeeper is one who holds himself out to the public as engaged in the business of keeping a house for the lodging and entertainment of travelers and passengers, their horses and attendants, for reasonable compensation. He is liable for any loss of property committed to his keeping, which any care or vigilance or diligence on his part could have prevented. If the defendant only occasionally entertained travelers for compensation, when it suited his pleasure to do so, and did not hold himself out to the public as the keeper of an inn, a house for the accommodation of the traveling public, then the defendant was only bound to take that ordinary care of property committed to his keeping that a prudent man usually takes of his own property of the same kind, and he would not be liable for a loss, unless it was shown that he had failed to use ordinary diligence in the care of property committed to him.

While this case was primarily concerned with liability for loss of property, it is instructive on the question of who is an innkeeper. In the opinion it was recognized that everyone who happens to accommodate a traveler, even if for compensation, is not necessarily to be held the keeper of an inn. The accommodation of travelers by the person must be in the nature of a business endeavor. In *Howth, supra,* the court continued in its opinion:

> There are numerous farmers situated on the public roads of the country, who occasionally, and even frequently, take in and accommodate travelers, and receive compensation for it, who are not innkeepers, and are not liable as such. It is not their business or occupation, nor do they prepare and fit up their establishments for it. They yield to the laws of hospitality in receiving and entertaining the stranger and the traveler, yet they cannot afford to do so without some compensation. This view of the subject the court also presented to the minds of the jury, by telling them, in substance, that if defendant only occasionally entertained travelers for compensation, when it suited his own pleasure, he did not thereby become an innkeeper.

There are today several types of establishments that provide lodging accommodations to members of the general population; there are hotels and motels, rooming houses, apartment houses, and boarding houses. Only hotels and motels, however, are truly descendants of the original inns and thus under the duty to accept all fit and proper persons who request lodging from them. The other establishments mentioned differ substantially in that their owners and operators may generally *choose* with whom they wish to contract for rooms. Usually the operator of a boarding house, rooming house, or apartment house will enter into a contract for a fixed period of time with the tenant. The operator generally accepts as tenants only those persons with whom he chooses to contract. This is a private, individual contract between operator and tenant. In contrast, hotels, motels, and inns hold themselves open to the *general public* rather than making specific individual contracts for a fixed rental period with only those persons with whom the operator chooses to deal. The guests in a hotel or motel are staying on a temporary basis. An individual building may, however, be operated as an inn and rooming house, with the relationship between the operators and various individuals staying in the building differing. The case of *Cedar Rapids Inv. Co. v. Commodore Hotel Co.* [205 Iowa 736, 218 N.W. 510 (1928)] recognized the significance of the temporary stay of the guest at an inn, stating that "it was the transient nature of the entertainment contracted for that distinguished the innkeeper from the lodging house or boarding house keeper."

The operator of a rooming house merely agrees to provide lodging accommodations to those with whom he wishes to deal, usually entering into special contracts for his compensation and the length of stay. A rooming house is not necessarily a public place where any fit person has a right to demand lodging. In contrast, an inn or hotel is a public place and has been defined as such in *City of Independence v. Richardson* [232 P. 1044 (Kan. 1925)]:

> . . . a business institution which is held out to the public as a house where all travelers and strangers or other transient persons having means of payment, and of proper demeanor and fair repute, who choose to patronize it, must be received and accommodated, to its capacity, without any previous agreement for accommodation or agreement as to duration of their stay.

The inn of prior years was the predecessor of today's hotel. Hotel, as a word, came into general use in our vocabulary quite some time ago. It generally came to denote a larger inn of a superior quality. A good discussion of the word's origin, from the case of *Cromwell v. Stephens* [2 Daly 15, 3 Abbot's Prac. (New Series) 26 (Ct. C.P.N.Y. Co. 1867)] follows:

> . . . the word hotel came into use in England by the general introduction in London, after 1760, of the kind of establishment that was then common in Paris, called an *hotel garni,* a large house, in which furnished apartments were let by the day, week, or month. In Barclay's Dictionary, 1872, in the first edition of Walker, 1791, and in Sheridan's Dictionary, 1795, hotel is given as the proper pronunciation of *hostel,* an inn; and in the dictionaries of Jones, 1798, and of Perry, 1805, it is incorporated as an English word, and is defined in the latter to be "an inn, having elegant lodgings and accommodations for gentlemen and genteel families." Todd, 1814, defines it to be "a lodging house for the accommodation of occasional lodgers, who are supplied with apartments hired by the night or week." The definition given by Knowles, 1835, is simply "a lodging house." By Smart, 1836, "a lodging house or inn." Beid, 1845, "an inn or a lodging house." Boaz, 1848, "an inn," and by Dr. Latham in his edition of Johnson's Dictionary, "an inn of a superior kind."
>
> The word was introduced into this country about 1797. Before that time houses for the entertainment of travelers in this city were at first called inns, and afterward taverns and coffee-houses. In 1794, an association, organized upon the principle of a tontine, erected in Wall Street what was then a very superior house for the accommodation of travelers, called the Tontine Coffee-house; the success of which led to the formation of another company for the erection of one upon a still more extensive scale in Broadway. This structure, which was called the

> Tontine Tavern, was built about 1796, upon the site of what had been a famous tavern or coffee-house in colonial times, and from the extensive accommodation it afforded, and the superior character of its appointments, it was then, and for many years afterward, the most celebrated establishment of the kind in the country. There was at that period a rage for everything French. The city was filled with refugees from France and from the French West India possessions, whose residence among us produced a great change in our social habits, amusements, and tastes, while a fierce party strife prevailed between those who advocated the principles of the French Revolution and those who condemned them. The French national airs were sung in the streets; men mounted the tricolor cockade; and the proprietors of the new tavern, falling in with the popular current, gave a French name to their establishment, by changing it from the Tontine Tavern to the City Hotel. The new word was afterward adopted by the proprietors of other houses for the entertainment of travelers in this and neighboring cities, and becoming general, found its way into American dictionaries. Allison, one of the earliest of American lexicographers, 1813, defines it to be "an inn of a high grade, a respectable tavern." Webster calls it "a house for entertaining strangers or travelers," and says that "it was formerly a house for genteel strangers or lodgers," but that "the name is now (1840) given to any inn." Worcester's definition (1846) is "a superior lodging-house with the accommodations of an inn; a public house; a genteel inn; an inn" and in the last edition of Webster, 1864, there is given an addition to the previous general definition: "An inn; a public house, especially one of some style or pretensions."
>
> It is to be deduced from the origin and history of the word, and the exposition that has been given of it by English and American lexicographers, that a hotel, in this country, is what in France was known as a *hostellerie,* and in England as a common inn of that superior class usually found in cities and large towns. A common inn is defined by Bacon to be a house for the entertainment of travelers and passengers, in which lodging and necessities are provided for them and for their horses and attendants.

As indicated above, a hotel came to denote a lodging establishment that was typically larger and of a superior quality. The City Hotel, as noted, was a prime example, as was the Tremont House in Boston, which opened in 1829. Both establishments sought to furnish superior accommodations and service to their guests. While originally hotels furnished food service for their guests and stabling accommodations for the traveler's horses, this is obviously not necessary today. Changing times and manner of travel no longer make this vital; all that is required is that lodging accommodations be provided for transient travelers.

With changing times, and especially changes in the major forms of transportations, there have been alterations in the physical form and setting of many hotels. Over the past several decades the private automobile has increased dramatically in importance as a means of transportation for millions of people. Largely as a result of this and thus the increasing number of persons traveling by automobile, we have seen the rise of the "motorist's hotel" or "motel." The opinion in *Schermer v. Fremar Corp.* [36 N.J. Super 46, 114 A.2d 757 (1955)] in part recognized the rise of the motel:

> It is of common knowledge that in the year 1930 motels were practically unheard of. Since 1944, with the great use of automobiles, there has been a tremendous development throughout the entire United States in the construction of buildings which furnish lodging accommodations for transients and which buildings are denominated motels. . . . These motels have filled a required need for housing accommodations for transients, making available to them accommodations quite generally more conveniently located for access by the traveling public than the normal hotel, and having greater facilities or accommodations for parking automobiles immediately adjacent to the building itself. The mode of operation of the average motel results as well in a great deal of "self-service" on the part of the guests and a reduction in the cost to the guest by way of gratuities. . . . In modern usage it may be generally regarded that establishments which furnish lodging to transients, although designated motels, may be deemed hotels. The word "motel" generally denotes a small hotel where lodgings are available for hire, with a minimum of personal service being furnished by the proprietor.

Thus the inns of yesteryear evolved into the hotels, and somewhat later the motels, of today. While today's hotels and motels, like the inns of years gone by, are privately owned and operated business establishments, they nonetheless have a "public" character as did the inn. By opening their doors to the public and soliciting the public's patronage they have given up the right to choose arbitrarily whom among the public they will serve. All fit and proper persons requesting accommodations must be served if accommodations are available.

While being generally receptive to members of the public, a hotel or motel may not refuse to accommodate a person applying for lodging because of that person's race, color, religion, or national origin. (See 42 U.S.C.A. § 2000 in Appendix A of this text.) The federal legislation prohibiting such discrimination applies to most hotels and motels but does not apply to private clubs or establishments that are not generally open to the public. The federal law prohibiting such discrimination has been held to apply even though it could be argued that a motel's operation was purely local. [*Heart of Atlanta Motel Inc. v. U.S.* 85 S.Ct. 348, 379 U.S. 241, 13 L.Ed.2d 258 (Ga. 1964).]

State laws typically restate the federal positions with respect to prohibiting racial discrimination and often prohibit discrimination on other bases, such as physical disability. They also, however, often state the operator's right to refuse service to truly objectional persons. An example of such is Florida Statute 509.092, which reads as follows:

> Public lodging establishments and public food service establishments are private enterprises, and the operator of a public lodging establishment or a public food service establishment has the right to refuse accommodations or service to any person who is objectionable or undesirable to the operator, but such refusal shall not be based upon race, creed, color, sex, physical disability or national origin.

As was true of the inn, the operator of the hotel or motel may legitimately refuse lodging facilities to one who is unfit. It is realistically only an arbitrary determination of unfitness that is objectionable. The operator of a lodging establishment would in fact appear to have an obligation to his guests to refrain from accommodating those members of the public who would pose a hazard to other guests. Certainly, pragmatically, an inn must keep one guest from unduly disturbing others. Often one may find that the law specifically recognizes the operator's right to refuse service or accommodations on the grounds of intoxification or other undesirable conduct. A further example is presented in part by Florida Statute 509.142:

> The operator of a public lodging establishment or public food service establishment may refuse accommodations or service to any person whose conduct on the premises of the establishment displays intoxication, immorality, profanity, lewdness or brawling; who indulges in language or conduct such as to disturb the peace or comfort of other guests, who engages in illegal or disorderly conduct; . . .

Whether or not to refuse service or accommodations to one applying for them is thus of necessity somewhat of a judgment call on the part of the hotel operator. So long as there is a legitimate reason for doing so he should bear no liability for this action. It does of course require the exercise of common sense and good judgment and is heavily dependent upon the factual setting of situations.

Now that we have examined the basic quasi-public nature of hotels and motels and the attendant obligation of them to serve the public it is desirable to consider next some basic concepts of legal liability. If one person is to be held legally liable for alleged injury caused to another it is necessary that there be a legal basis for such liability. This is the subject of Chapter 2.

CHAPTER 2

THE LAW AND LEGAL SYSTEM

TO better understand the concepts to be discussed in the next chapter it is desirable to look briefly at the legal system in general and its background. From personal experience as both an attorney and college professor teaching business law the author has found that when the layman thinks of the "law," or when the college student begins a study in business "law" both typically bring with them a preconceived belief that the law consists simply of a set of rules governing conduct, rules that are black and white, clear-cut, wherein there are absolute rights and wrongs. By memorizing these rules one can thus learn the "law." Unfortunately, good guys don't always wear white hats and bad guys black ones. Things in the real world are not nearly so simple, there are few absolutes, and black and white often yield to shades of gray. The law is a very complex subject, mirroring the very complexities of our modern society. While stability is sought so that the law may be known and expected to remain relatively constant, change also occurs. Indeed, while stability is desirable, the law must also have flexibility to meet the new challenges of changing times. What might once have been held to be the recognized law may no longer be, due to changes in court decisions or the enactments of legislative bodies. Yet there are many fundamental concepts and principles in our law that have spanned centuries and that will endure for centuries more.

Contrary to the belief of some persons, the law is not some staid, musty old collection of rigid rules and regulations that hinder our individual freedom of action. Rather it is really a vibrant, living creation of man's mind given to reaching for that most sacred goal of achieving justice among us mortals. In this country we as a people have dedicated ourselves to the concept that we are a nation ruled by *laws,* not men, and even the government and its highest officials are subject to our law. In this is found the strength of our system.

In the United States there are really fifty-one slightly differing legal systems. This is the result of the structure of the government. The country has a federal government with limited powers rather than a national government. The nation is a union of many states, each essentially a sovereign state in many respects with its own court system, which has jurisdiction within the confines of the state. Each legislature of each state has the right to enact laws binding within the bounds of the state. The Federal Constitution puts certain limitations on state power in that the federal government is given certain powers to the exclusion of the states, and of course the states cannot infringe upon basic rights guaranteed in the Constitution. If there develops a conflict between federal legislation on a subject and state legislation with respect to the same matter, then the federal law will prevail under the supremacy clause of the Constitution.

It is common to hear people speak of the "law." When doing so it is beneficial to consider the source of the "law" of which they are speaking. There are many places where one can look for the law, one being to look at the constitutions of the individual states and the Federal Constitution. These are fundamental documents establishing the form and structure of government, basic powers thereof, and basic rights of individuals. State constitutions are subordinate to the United States Constitution, but otherwise they are superior to other sources of the law within a particular state. They are the cornerstones of the law.

A second source of the law is the written laws enacted by a legislative body such as a state legislature. These are referred to as *statutes*. Local legislative bodies, such as city councils, also enact written laws, but they have only local application and are referred to as ordinances. Statutes apply statewide.

Individual state legislatures enact statutory law on many and varying subjects, which laws are binding within the confines of the state. Statutes on any given subject matter may often vary somewhat from state to state because of the varied views of the lawmakers in different states. The following is an example that might be relevant to any hotel or motel operating a bar or lounge. A statute in state A may allow persons who are eighteen years of age or older to purchase and consume alcoholic beverages, while in state B persons must be twenty-one years of age to do so lawfully. While in state A the eighteen year old may legally purchase a drink, he cannot do so when he enters the geographic boundary of state B. He must respect and comply with the law of state B while in that state. He cannot seek to purchase alcohol in state B by arguing that he could do so in his home state A. Statutes of state A are the law only within the confines of state A; they have no extraterritorial effect. Even within state A they must not conflict with federal law on the subject, or the state constitution. As each state in the Union is a sovereign state, the enactments of its legislature and the jurisdiction of its courts extend only to the boundaries of the state.

Our society has changed and become more complex over the years and so have business in general and our individual business relationships. Our economy is normally characterized as a free market economy, and it predominantly is. It has never been a truly *laissez faire* economy, however; to one extent or another, at one level or another, government has always been involved with the economy. It early became obvious that some degree of government involvement in the economy was desirable and necessary, often to prevent the development of undesirable and unfair practices between businesses. Much of the early involvement of the federal government in the latter part of the nineteenth century was geared toward restraining the formation of monopolies and trusts, as a matter of public policy both being considered adverse to the public interest.

As the complexities of the business world increased it became more difficult for legislative bodies to legislate directly some problem areas involving very technical questions. A result has been the enactment of legislation, both at the federal and state level, creating various administrative agencies, such agencies being given responsibility for regulating various aspects of business and commerce. One of the earliest of the federal administrative agencies was the Interstate Commerce Commission (ICC), which was created by legislation enacted by the Congress in 1887. Other agencies created later were modeled after the ICC. State agencies are similar in nature to those of the federal government.

A third important source of law today is the rules and regulations of these agencies or *administrative law*. Through the legislation that created them, administrative agencies have generally been given the power to promulgate rules and regulations necessary to carry out their regulatory responsibility. Their rules and regulations, when properly enacted, generally have the force and effect of law. In years past the right of administrative agencies to promulgate rules having the effect of law was challenged in the courts. Opponents argued that to allow an agency such power was an improper delegation of its duty by the legislative body responsible. The argument was essentially that under the Constitution the duty to enact laws was given to the legislative body and that it could not properly delegate this to a body it created. The right of agencies to enact rules and regulations with the effect of law was, however, upheld in the courts. Some standards or guidelines must be provided for the agency though. Realistically, in today's modern and complex world of business it is very unlikely that most legislative bodies would have the technical expertise or competence necessary adequately to regulate many complicated areas of commerce. Constitutionally, our government is separated into three branches: legislative, executive, and judicial. By creating a "separation of powers" in the government the Founding Fathers believed that each branch of government would act as a check or balance against the undue and potentially dangerous concentration of power in any one branch. It must be remembered that at the time the Constitution was being framed the country had just recently wrested its independence from another power that had exercised absolute authority over it. People had been alarmed by abuse of power by the prior governing authorities and infringement upon what they felt were their rights as subjects of the Crown. The new nation adopted the then somewhat novel idea that all men were created equal and possessed fundamental rights. Real concern with the potential for abuse of power by the new government led to the demand that it be established in such a form to prevent this from occurring. Demand also was made that the Constitution recognize certain fundamental rights.

Administrative agencies of government are unique in that they often possess powers found in each of the three separate branches of government. That is to say, they often promulgate rules and regulations having the force and effect of law, and they enforce these same rules and regulations much as the executive department enforces laws. Often agencies would also function in a quasi-judicial manner by interpreting their own regulations; today, however, this is more often within the province of independent administrative law judges. One seeking relief from adverse rulings of agencies must normally follow the prescribed route of administrative appeals, first giving the agency an opportunity to correct any errors made. Ultimately redress may be sought in the courts.

A fourth source of law is found in *case law,* the rulings and decisions of the courts. A court may be defined as a tribunal established by government to hear and decide disputes brought before it. While there are many possible methods of settling untested questions between two persons, the procedure of presenting them to a court for settlement is probably the fairest and most just of these. In many cases a court will be called upon to make a ruling interpreting a statute, regulation, or constitution in the course of judging a case. Such a ruling by the court will then become a part of the law on the subject concerned. In many other instances there may not be any statute considered controlling to be interpreted and the court must then refer to the common law. On occasion a unique question of first impression may be presented when there are no prior case decisions on similar points.

Due to its tremendous influence on our own law and legal system it is beneficial to look briefly at the beginnings of the English court system. The Normans conquered England in the year 1066 and very shortly thereafter set about attempting to unite the country under Norman rule. Part of the plan for unifying the country involved creation of the Curia Regis, or the king's court. Before this time disputes had been settled typically by reference to the applicable local custom; with the establishment of the king's court the attempt to unify customs and law in England began. Decisions of the courts and the rules established were the beginning of the common law of England, later largely adopted in the United States and elsewhere in the English-speaking world.

In making decisions it became customary for courts to refer to prior court decisions in similar types of cases for guidance in settling issues and questions. Such prior case decisions became *precedents* to be followed in subsequent similar cases. This rule of following the concepts and principles established in earlier cases became known as the doctrine of *stare decisis* and has proven to be exceptionally valuable not only to the English legal system but to our own as well. With courts following established precedents the law is more just, and there is less tendency for any individual court to make an arbitrary decision. The doctrine lends greater stability to the law.

Stability in the law is highly desirable so that one can govern individual and business decisions based upon reasonable knowledge of what the law holds on the subject. However, times change and thus the law must be flexible as well as stable. A concept that is no longer appropriate for the times may be overturned by the courts and a new principle of law or a modified one stated. As an example, under the common law a charitable institution was often held to be immune from a lawsuit resulting from a tort committed by one of its servants or employees. This concept of charitable immunity has generally been given up by court decisions in the various states. The reason for the initial existence of rule has been considered to have since vanished; in the past such institutions had very limited assets with which to satisfy any such claims, but today general liability insurance is available. [See *Flagiello v. Pennsylvania Hospital* 208 A.2d 193 (Pa. 1965).] In the United States the highest court in each state, by its decisions, sets precedent within that state. Its decisions are not binding upon the courts of other states, but its reasoning in a case may often be pursuasive, especially if the subject has not previously been considered by the courts of the other state. Many basic legal principles are, in concept, generally accepted by the state court systems, and of course decisions of the United States Supreme Court are binding upon all courts in the land.

As previously mentioned, courts are frequently called upon to interpret statutes, regulations, or constitutions. The power of the courts to determine whether or not a law is contrary to the Constitution is known as the power of *judicial review* and was first established in the landmark case of *Marbury v. Madison* [5. U.S. (1 Cranch) 137, 2 L.Ed. 60 (1803)]. The Supreme Court stated:

> It is emphatically the province and duty of the Judicial Department to say what the law is. Those who apply the rule to a particular case, must of necessity expound and interpret that rule. If two laws conflict with

> each other, the courts must decide on the operation of each. So if the law be in opposition to the Constitution if both the law and the Constitution apply to a particular case, so that the court must either decide that case conformable to the law, disregarding the Constitution; or conformably to the Constitution, disregarding the law; the court must determine which of these conflicting rules governs the case. This is of the very essence of judicial duty.

The Court recognized its right to determine the constitutionality of laws and that the Constitution is the supreme law of the land in the United States. Courts henceforth stood as guardians against the enactment of laws that were violative of the Constitution.

In the United States there are both state court systems and the federal courts. Without going into an extended discussion of the circumstances under which a lawsuit may be filed in each, suffice it here to say that very often a suit may be filed and prosecuted in either state or federal court. Initially the choice of legal forums belongs to the *plaintiff,* that party claiming injury who institutes the lawsuit. The party being sued, the *defendant,* may under some circumstances remove a case initially filed in a state court to a federal court. The law applied by either court is the same; it is usually simply the plaintiff's choice of courts when either would be appropriate. The following discussion will concern a state court system, however.

All courts cannot hear and decide all cases. Before a court may proceed with a case filed before it, the court must have *jurisdiction* to do so. Jurisdiction is the power of a court to hear and decide a case. Some courts have *original jurisdiction,* that is to say that these are courts in which lawsuits are first filed and heard. These courts are trial courts. Other courts do not function as trial courts, but their purpose is to review the proceedings of a trial court to make certain that no error was committed and that the law was properly applied. These courts are referred to as *appellate* courts, and they have *appellate jurisdiction,* the power to review actions of trial courts. If an appeals court finds error in a trial court proceeding it may send the case back for a retrial or further proceedings in accordance with its instructions. The trial court must follow the ruling of the appeals court.

In most states there is currently something of a three-tier court structure, with basic trial courts at the base, then intermediate appeals courts, and finally the highest court of the state, often called the state supreme court. The structure is as follows:

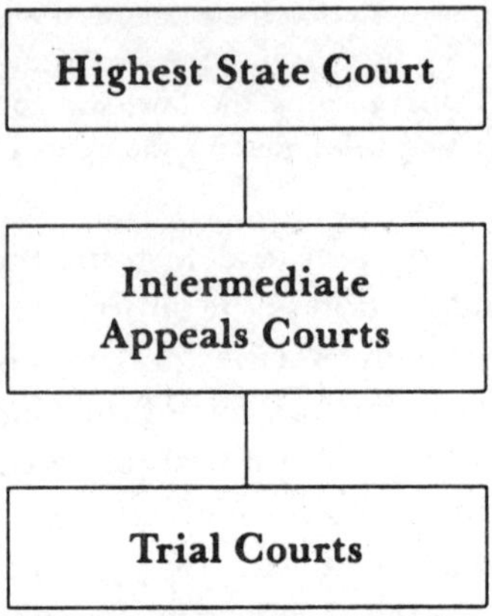

The highest state court has power to review rulings by the intermediate appeals courts, and its rulings and decisions stand as precedent to be followed by all lower courts in the state. This explanation of the structure of a state court system is, admittedly, somewhat oversimplified. Depending upon the state there may be other courts; it should also be noted that a functional equivalent, such as a basic trial court, may be known by different names in different states.

Courts may also be of *general* or *limited jurisdiction.* For example, in some states there are courts with limited jurisdiction that hear only certain types of cases, such as probate matters or domestic relations cases. Sometimes separate courts are established to hear only criminal cases.

With a basic concept of the typical court system established let us now consider very briefly how a lawsuit begins and proceeds. A lawsuit begins with the injured or complaining party, the *plaintiff,* filing what is normally called a *complaint.* The complaint is filed by the plaintiff with the clerk of the appropriate court. The clerk will assign a case number and a judge will be assigned the case. The clerk creates a file for the case in which all original pleadings and papers will be filed. A *summons* is issued and together with a copy of the complaint will be served on the defendant in the action. A very simple complaint is shown on page 24, followed by a summons. The summons is a form summons and has been left blank; in an actual case the pertinent information would be filled in. The complaint basically states the claim that the plaintiff has against the defendant and includes a demand for some type of relief, usually money damages.

Due process of law requires that when a defendant is sued he or she be given notice of the suit and the opportunity to defend against it. This is the reason the summons and a copy of the complaint are required to be served upon the defendant. By so doing the court acquires jurisdiction over the defendant to proceed. Normally the summons and complaint are served by the sheriff or a deputy by delivering a copy of these papers personally to the defendant, although in certain situations it may be possible to use alternative methods.

Once the defendant has been served there is a time limit within which an answer or some other response must be filed with the court. If the defendant chooses to do nothing within this time period the plaintiff may seek to have a default entered and proceed to seek judgement. Usually, though, the defendant will respond and the case will proceed. Many procedural steps may be followed, and there may be a number of hearings on various motions made during the course of a suit, but ultimately the matter will usually reach trial if a settlement is not reached by the parties. The case may be tried only to a judge, but more commonly plaintiff, defendant, or both will have demanded a jury trial, which is usually their right.

After presentation of evidence and both sides of the case the issues will go to the jury for decision, with the court having given appropriate instructions to the jury on the law. The jury will then return a verdict in the case. If a party believes error has been committed in the course of the trial then an appeal may be filed for review of the case by an appellate court. Assuming that no appeal is filed the judgment entered will stand. Obtaining a judgment and enforcing one are often two different things, as many a "victorious" plaintiff has discovered. Unfortunately it may turn out that a judgment obtained against a defendant is, practically speaking, uncollectible, as the defendant may have little if any assets with which to pay the judgment and often there may be no insurance coverage that might apply to cover the judgment. Realistically this is one matter the plaintiff must carefully weigh before deciding to file and pursue a lawsuit. If the defendant has no assets then the plaintiff may simply have to be satisfied with recording the judgment and hoping that it may prove to be collectible at a later date.

This outline of the proceedings in a lawsuit is very brief and somewhat oversimplified, but it does serve to introduce some of the fundamentals. In Chapter 3 we shall examine some basic concepts of legal liability, reasons why one party may be held liable to another for injuries sustained.

IN THE CIRCUIT COURT OF THE 17TH JUDICIAL CIRCUIT IN AND FOR BROWARD COUNTY, FLORIDA

Case No.

JOHN DOE)
Plaintiff)
vs.
ACME MOTEL INC. a)
Florida corporation)
Defendant)

Complaint

JOHN DOE, Plaintiff, sues ACME MOTEL INC., a Florida corporation, defendant, and alleges:

1. This is an action for damages in excess of Five Thousand Dollars.

2. JOHN DOE, a resident of Anytown, Florida, was on March 8, 198_, a registered and paying guest at the motel owned and operated by defendant located at 115 North Street, Dolphin Beach, Florida.

3. On the above mentioned date Plaintiff, while walking across the floor of the motel lobby, slipped and fell. Plaintiff's fall was directly caused by the negligence of the Defendant in allowing a puddle of water to have accumulated on the floor of said motel lobby. Defendant knew of the existence of such dangerous condition or in the exercise of reasonable care should have known, and failed to rectify the situation or to warn Plaintiff of same.

4. As a direct result of defendant's negligence Plaintiff was injured, has sustained loss of wages as a result of said injury, has been forced to incur expense for medical treatment and will in the future, has suffered pain and will in the future, and has sustained permanency in such injury.

Plaintiff demands trial by jury of all issues triable in this case.

Wherefore, Plaintiff demands judgment for damages against Defendant and further relief which the Court deems proper.

Martin Winner Esq.
Attorney for Plaintiff
100 Elm Street
Dolphin Beach, Florida

IN THE CIRCUIT COURT OF THE SEVENTEENTH JUDICIAL CIRCUIT
BROWARD COUNTY, FLORIDA

CASE NO.

Plaintiff,

— vs —

Defendant,

SUMMONS

THE STATE OF FLORIDA:

To All and Singular the Sheriffs of said State:

YOU ARE HEREBY COMMANDED to serve this summons and a copy of the complaint or petition in this action on defendant

Each defendant is required to serve written defenses to the complaint or petition on

Plaintiff's attorney, whose address is

within 20 days after service of this summons on that defendant, exclusive of the day of service, and to file the original of the defenses with the clerk of this court either before service on plaintiff's attorney or immediately thereafter. If a defendant fails to do so, a default will be entered against that defendant for the relief demanded in the complaint or petition.

WITNESS my hand and the Seal of said Court

As Clerk of said Court

by________________________

CHAPTER 3

LOSS AND LEGAL LIABILITY

RISK is uncertainty whether or not loss will occur. Everyday individuals and businesses are faced with risk, the possibility of numerous incidents occurring that might result in the individual or business sustaining some type of loss. Fire may break out, destroying a home or burning down a business establishment. An automobile accident may occur in which property is damaged or life lost. An employee of a business may cause injury to a third party, thereby possibly exposing the employer to liability for the injuries. Life is such that one is confronted daily with the *possibility* of sustaining many types of losses due to many different causative factors. What one is usually unsure of is whether or not the loss *will* occur, the probability. There are some incidents that are very unlikely to occur; others are almost certain to at some time.

As individuals and businesses faced with risk we must develop strategies to contend with it. There are some instances in which a risk of loss may be avoided. An extreme example follows: The risk of loss of merchandise due to a fire in a business establishment may be *avoided* by not going into business, or if already in business, by closing. Obviously, this is practically an unsatisfactory choice. There are many risks that simply cannot reasonably be avoided. To avoid a risk of loss of merchandise by not opening a business is an absurdity.

Practically, if many risks cannot be avoided, then some other concept of dealing with the chance of loss must be developed. One method of contending with risk, which is often extremely useful, is attempting to *minimize* it, to reduce the probability of it occurring. In the preceding example there are many steps and precautions that may be taken to reduce the likelihood of a fire or at least diminish its severity. In flammables, if stored at all, can be stored in a safe manner, perhaps restricted to a fireproof area. A building sprinkler system can be installed in the business premises. Employees can be instructed in fire safety and encouraged to exercise prevention, and general operating procedures of the business may be examined from a safety standpoint.

Even though some risks are minimized, many incidents causing loss may still occur. The individual or business may therefore simply accept the remaining possibility of loss and, if it occurs, absorb the loss. This is self-insuring in a sense.

Another possibility is that the risk of loss may be shifted to someone else. The primary way in which this is done is by obtaining a policy of *insurance* against losses, thus shifting part or all of the risk to a professional risk taker. When a policy of insurance is purchased, the purchaser (insured) is required to pay a premium to the insurance company (insurer) for the protection extended. The insured is accepting a certain known loss (paying the premium) in exchange for protection against an uncertain but possible future loss of greater magnitude. The premium charged by the insurer depends upon several factors, most important the likelihood of the loss occurring and the exposure of the insurer if it does. Vast amounts of statistical data on losses are collected and analyzed by insurers to determine probabilities of losses and premiums to be charged.

Some losses may be sustained due to actions of other parties for which such parties should be held liable in damages to the one injured. At other times injury may result from an unavoidable accident or may be due wholly or in part to fault of the party injured themself. In such a situation there may be no third party to be held liable. Insurance coverage may still provide some protection. The main concern of this chapter will be, however, a brief discussion of some theories of legal liability, *why* one party should be held liable for injuries or losses sustained by another.

There are many "wrongs" that may be committed by one party against another, and the seriousness of them varies. Some wrongs are considered crimes; a *crime* is a violation of law that is punished because it is considered an offense against the state, against society itself. If people are to live together in an organized and civilized society it is necessary and desirable that certain conduct be prevented as being detrimental to the interests of the society itself. This conduct, which is prohibited by declaring it an offense against the state, would be termed criminal conduct. Those who would then engage in such conduct are prosecuted by the state. As an example, an assault and battery committed by A upon B would be a crime. Not only is B injured, but this type of conduct on the part of A is an offense also against all of society. Society itself has a valid interest in preventing such conduct or, if it occurs, punishing for it. To do otherwise would invite anarchy and injustice.

Other conduct may be a wrong with respect to the party the conduct is directed to, but not necessarily against the state. A *tort* is a wrong arising out of a violation of a private duty outside of contract. As an example, if A is taking a walk and swinging a stick, A may accidently hit and injure B, who is also walking on the sidewalk. Though the action of swinging the stick was lawful, A had a duty imposed upon him to conduct himself in such a manner that his actions in swinging the stick would not cause injury to others. A may have violated this duty by thus injuring B and may be liable to B. The same conduct *may* be both a tort and a crime. In the example above if A had intentionally struck B for no valid reason, intending to injure B, the act of A would be a crime also. The reason for given conduct and the intent of the person are often of great importance.

Most persons of reason and ordinary sensibilities could agree that generally an individual should be held responsible for his actions that cause injury to another. Legally this forms one basis for recovery of damages suffered as the result of an injury. The law has long held those *intentionally* causing harm liable for their actions. Thus if A should intentionally beat B with a stick B may sue and recover damages against A, assuming that A has no valid reason for striking B, such as self-defense against acts of B. In such a situation B could recover actual damages such as physicians' costs incurred, drugs, lost wages, and pain and suffering resulting from injuries sustained. Also in all probability B may recover *punitive* damages against A. Punitive damages are those damages awarded a plaintiff that are over and above the actual damages sustained by the plaintiff. They are also sometimes referred to as *exemplary* damages and are usually awarded in civil cases only where it is shown that a defendant has acted willfully and with malice. The purpose of such an award to the plaintiff is to punish the defendant and to make an example of him, thus to discourage similar conduct in the future on his part or others.

Another basis of liability is found in the concept of *absolute liability.* Responsibility for harm is being imposed without regard to whether there has been any negligence or intent to cause harm on the part of the defendant. Simply because the defendant chose to engage in the activity he is held liable for any injury caused to others resulting from the activity. The classic case is that of blasting. If contractor A blasts and debris is hurled onto B's property, causing damage, A is usually held responsible for the damage even though he did not intend to cause harm to B and even though he had taken reasonable safeguards.

Certain activities are such that there is a great risk of harm to others when engaging in them, yet such activities are frequently necessary and so they are not outlawed. The law then often holds one engaging in such activity absolutely liable for resulting injuries. With respect to the types of activities that give rise to absolute liability the law of each state must be examined; aside from the example of blasting, storing dangerous chemicals in a densely populated area or keeping a wild animal as a pet in a populated area could be other examples. Sometimes state statutes will come close to imposing absolute liability; for example see Florida Statute § 767.04 with respect to the liability of a dog owner for dog bites wherein there are only limited defenses to the owner when his dog bites another person.

A third major basis of legal liability is found in the concept of *negligence;* in fact by far the majority of tort actions are based on a theory of negligence. The basic concept of negligence is that each individual member of society has a duty to conduct his or her affairs in a manner that avoids injury to others. The individual must conduct himself or herself in his or her affairs as an ordinary reasonable and prudent man would in the same or under similar circumstances. This "reasonable man" standard is objective yet flexible. The standard of conduct required in a given situation is not necessarily that of an "average" person but rather is that of a reasonable and prudent man.

For a defendant in a lawsuit to be found negligent with respect to his or her actions in a given situation certain things must be shown. Initially it must be established that the defendant owed a duty of care to the plaintiff with respect to actions of the defendant. Second, the defendant by his action or inaction must have breached this duty of care imposed upon him. Third, as a direct and proximate result of the breach of duty by defendant the plaintiff must have been caused injury and suffered damages. If any of these elements of the case are absent then the defendant should not be found to have been negligent under the circumstances.

It is beneficial to look at an example when discussing the concept of negligence. A hypothetical situation involving a slip and fall by John Doe, a guest, in the lobby of the Acme Motel (fictional) should be useful as an illustration. Should the motel be held liable to the plaintiff Doe? The answer to this question depends upon the facts of the case.

Businesses are *not* normally held to insure the safety of their invitees, the doctrine of absolute liability previously discussed not applying. A business establishment does, however, have a duty imposed upon it to exercise reasonable care in making and keeping its premises reasonably safe for invitees. This duty is breached if the business creates a dangerous condition or fails to correct it when the business has knowledge that it exists, or with the exercise of reasonable care it should have had such knowledge or fails to warn of it. Retail businesses frequently have problems involving slips and falls by customers. Before the store is to be held liable it must of course be shown that the store is in fact at fault, as is true of essentially any business open to the public. It is insufficient merely to establish that the accident occurred on the business premises. In *Perminas v. Montgomery Ward & Co.* [328 N.E.2d 290 (Ill. 1975)] the court stated this clearly:

> We wish to emphasize that we "firmly adhere to the rule that a storekeeper is not the insurer of his customer's safety." We do not hold, by this decision, that a storekeeper is negligent simply because he displays small objects with wheels which could possibly be dropped on the floor and cause someone to fall. Liability must be founded on fault; and that fault is found here in the evidence that defendant, after receiving notice that a particular product was creating a dangerous situation, failed to return its premises to a safe condition or warn its customers of the existence of the danger.

In the preceding motel example if the plaintiff John Doe slips and falls because of a puddle of water or other object on the lobby floor, which the motel either caused to be there and/or allowed to remain there without cleaning it up, the motel will very probably be held to have breached the duty of care imposed upon it to make its premises reasonably safe for its guests. A business should exercise reasonable care in not allowing a known hazard to continue and should in fact take proper steps to determine the existence of hazards and dangerous conditions. Periodic inspection of premises is usually desirable; many retail businesses maintain a "sweep schedule" where an employee will periodically check the premises, looking for and cleaning up spills and debris. It might be here noted that the duty owed by a business to a licensee (one coming onto the premises for his own benefit) or a trespasser is somewhat different.

The last required element would be that the motel's breach of duty was the direct and proximate cause of John Doe's injury. In this example it should be so considered. With exercise of reasonable care the puddle should have been discovered and cleaned, the hazard eliminated, and Doe's injury by falling avoided. By breaching its duty of care the motel is responsible for the injury. In tort law causation is sometimes a problem; without causation the defendant is not liable.

In order for the plaintiff to recover he must of course have suffered some injury or loss. If in the example no injury or loss occurs then the plaintiff can hardly seek a recovery against the defendant. Often this question of injury presents a thorny issue in a lawsuit. Determining the existence or nonexistence of injury and its extent can at times be very difficult and require extensive medical evidence. In cases alleging personal injury there are numerous expenses recoverable by the plaintiff. Bills of physicians, hospital expenses, prescriptions, necessary sick room equipment, wages lost due to lost work time, pain and suffering, permanency of the injury, all and more may be considered in awarding damages to the plaintiff. The plaintiff must, of course, prove these losses and not simply allege them.

In a negligence suit there are defenses available to the defendant. These may relieve the defendant of liability or at least operate in some cases to reduce any damages recoverable by the plaintiff. It may be shown that by his own actions the plaintiff was guilty of *con-*

tributory negligence, that is, he did something that was at least partially the cause of his own injury. In many jurisdictions contributory negligence has operated to prohibit the plaintiff from *any* recovery against the defendant. This could operate very unfairly in some cases and lead to an unjust result, especially when the plaintiff bears very little fault. Doctrines such as *last clear chance* have developed in the law to mitigate the harshness of the concept of contributory negligence. Under this doctrine the plaintiff, though partially to blame himself, can still proceed in an action against the defendant if the defendant had the last opportunity to avoid the harm or injury and did not do so. Another defense frequently used is *assumption of the risk.* Thus when one knowingly enters an area of danger he cannot recover as a result of another person's negligence.

Some states have moved away from contributory negligence and have adopted the concept of *comparative negligence* whereby a plaintiff's contributory negligence does not prohibit a recovery. Damages are apportioned between plaintiff and defendant. Damages that are found due to the plaintiff's *own* negligence are deducted from the total damages suffered before a recovery from defendant. There are variations with respect to application of comparative negligence.

This chapter has considered the question of loss and basic concepts of legal liability, examining these briefly. The following chapters will consider more specific topics concerning liability of motels and hotels.

CHAPTER 4

LOSS OF GUESTS' PROPERTY

COMMON LAW LIABILITY

VIRTUALLY all hotel or motel managers and front desk personnel have had the unfortunate experience of having a concerned, sometimes frantic, guest report the loss, theft, or disappearance of personal belongings while staying at the hotel or motel. Often after such initial report of loss the guest's concern may turn to anger and a demand for the establishment to "do something," usually compensate the guest for the loss. All too often when property disappears from a guest's room the allegation is raised that the property was of substantial value, anything from jewelry to cameras or firearms. Unfortunately the hotel or motel has no particular way to verify such allegations after the fact. An unpleasant situation too often develops for all involved.

Thus the issue of whether or not a hotel or motel operator is liable for loss of a guest's property and personal belongings frequently arises. Numerous situations may occur wherein property belonging to a guest disappears from his or her room or even perhaps from a hotel safety deposit box. Whether or not the operator of the establishment is held legally liable for the loss will depend largely upon the facts of the individual situation. Was the operator of the hotel or motel negligent with respect to causing the loss? Did the guest do something or fail to do something that contributed directly to the loss? What actually did cause the loss? What is the statutory law of the state with respect to innkeeper's liability for property loss? In determining whether or not the establishment is to be held legally liable for the loss these are some of the questions that must be answered. What an establishment is formally called, the name given to it, is not as important as the realities of its function. A person furnishing the services of a hotelkeeper has such status even though the word *hotel* is not used in the business name. It is the services offered and facilities available that are determinative. [*Lackman v. Department of Labor and Industries* 78 Wash.2d 212, 471 P.2d 82 (1970).]

Before further considering the scope of the hotel operator's responsibility for the property of his guests it is helpful to discuss the legal concept of a *bailment* because under the common law the innkeeper was considered an extraordinary bailee with respect to guests' property. The term bailment is one that typically is not familiar to the layman, yet the relationship that it represents is one in which the layman has many times previously been involved. A formal definition of the term is found in *Black's Law Dictionary,* Revised Fourth Edition:

> A delivery of goods or personal property, by one person to another, in trust for the execution of a special object upon or in relation to such goods, beneficial either to the bailor or bailee or both, and upon a contract, express or implied, to perform the trust and carry out such object, and thereupon either to redeliver the goods to the bailor or otherwise dispose of the same in conformity with the purpose of the trust.

The essence, then, of a bailment is that one person, the *bailor,* is entrusting possession of personal property to another person, the *bailee,* with the understanding that the identical property will be returned to the bailor or else disposed of according to instructions from the bailor. A bailment may be *gratuitous;* for example you loan this book to a friend to read. You are not deriving any particular benefit from the arrangement, but you do expect to have the book returned to you. A bailment may also be one for mutual benefit of bailor and bailee. An example would be when one rents a tool from a rental store. The tool must be returned, but the relationship is for the benefit of both parties, the person renting the tool having the use of it and the store being paid the rental charges. Leaving clothing to be dry cleaned is another familiar example of a bailment relationship.

In an ordinary bailment there are certain duties and responsibilities imposed upon both bailor and bailee. The bailor has the duty to inform the bailee of any known dangerous condition of the property and perhaps previously to have actively inspected it. The bailee has a duty to exercise reasonable care to protect and preserve the property while it is in his possession and to make no unauthorized use of the property. The bailor must normally expect the *ordinary* wear and tear associated with use of the property to occur. So long as the bailee exercises reasonable care of the property the bailor still assumes risk of loss or damage. Only if the bailee has failed to exercise reasonable care or was making an unauthorized use of the property that caused its damage is he held liable for loss of or injury to the property. Thus under the common law a bailee was *not* an insurer of the safety of property in an *ordinary* bailment. It should be noted here, however, that this common law responsibility could be expanded by contract. The bailee may agree to assuming a greater responsibility for the safety of the property while in his possession. Such may sometimes be found in formal rental agreements where the renter (bailee) assumes all responsibility for loss or damage to property while in his possession.

Under the common law a greater liability for the safety of property was imposed upon common carriers transporting goods and upon innkeepers than was the case in an ordinary bailment. With respect to innkeepers the innkeeper was virtually an insurer of the safety of his guests' property and was liable for losses suffered by the guest while *infra hospitium* (within the inn). It might be argued that taking property into a hotel or motel room by a guest does not technically create a bailment relationship between the guest and the hotel or motel. This is so because the hotelkeeper does not normally have knowledge of what specific articles are in the room and also because the hotelkeeper's "possession" of the property is not exclusive; the guest can move it. Yet the rule developed that the innkeeper was to be held liable for almost any loss of a guest's belongings while in the inn. This rule making the innkeeper liable was founded on considerations of public policy. It was intended to protect innocent travelers from dishonesty or negligence of an innkeeper or his servants, and its development was traced by the court in its opinion in the case of *Hanover Insurance Co. v. Alamo Motel* [264 N.W.2d 774 (Iowa 1978)]:

> The rule devolved from the Roman era and was designed to protect travel and commerce in times of highwaymen who were often in league with innkeepers:

> "Rigorous as this law may seem, and hard as it may actually be in some instances, it is, as Sir William Jones observes, founded on the principle of public utility, to which all private considerations ought to yield. Travelers, who must be numerous in a rich and commercial country, are obliged to rely almost implicitly on the good faith of innkeepers; and it would be almost impossible for them, in any given case, to make out proof of fraud or negligence in the landlord. The Roman praetor held innkeepers responsible for the goods of their guests, on the same principle of public utility. It was necessary, says Ulpian, in commenting on the edict of the praetor, to confide largely in the honesty of such men; and if they were not held very strictly to their duty they might yield to the temptation to commit a breach of trust. They were bound to answer for all losses, and damages happening even without their default, unless they were fatal losses, occurring from vis major or irresistible force." (–2 *Kent's Commentaries,* p. 975, 14th ed., 1896)

Thus the responsibility placed upon the innkeeper by the common law for the safety of his guests' property was indeed a very great responsibility. The innkeeper became the next thing to an insurer of the property. The same common law concept was expressed by a Pennsylvania court in *Buck v. Hankin* [217 Pa.Super. 262, 269 A.2d 344 (1970)], where in its opinion the court stated:

> A reading of the leading cases on the subject of an innkeeper's common law liability reveal that it was regarded as strict and absolute, not based on negligence. As early as 1869, our Supreme Court in Houser v. Tully 62 Pa. 92 (1869) reasoned: "The liability of an innkeeper arises from the nature of his employment. He holds out a general invitation to travelers to come to his house, and he receives a reward for his hospitality. The law, in return, imposes on him corresponding duties, one of which is, to protect the property of those whom he receives as guests.

Under the common law it was recognized, however, that certain occurrences were completely beyond the control of the innkeeper and thus if loss of property were caused by one of these the innkeeper was relieved of responsibility. These unusual occurrences were few in number. The innkeeper would be relieved of liability for loss of a guest's property if the loss resulted from an act of God, a public enemy, or the fault of the guest himself. [*Zurich Fire Ins. Co. of New York v. Weil* 259 S.W.2d 54 (Ky. App. 1953).] In the *Zurich* case the loss appeared to have been caused by an off duty hotel employee. The guest parked his auto in front of a hotel, went in, and registered as a guest. A bellboy then came out, took charge of the guest's baggage, and showed him to his room whereupon the guest asked about storage of his auto. The bellboy took the guest's keys and gave a claim check to him. The hotel had an arrangement with a private garage for the storing of guests' cars, but this was not made known to the guest. When the guest attempted to claim his auto the next day it was discovered that it was gone. Subsequently it was found, wrecked, apparently having been taken by an offduty hotel bellboy. Regardless of any arrangement the hotel itself had with the garage, the guest had been led to believe that the auto was being entrusted to the hotel, and the hotel was thus held responsible for the loss.

The three preceding situations, which would, under the common law, relieve the innkeeper from liability for loss of the guest's property, sometimes led to questions of their scope and what was included within them. If a guest in a hotel lost property because of being robbed while in the hotel, was the hotel responsible for the loss, or was this the act of a "public enemy" so as to relieve the hotel of liability to the guest? The court considered this question in *Johnston v. Mobile Hotel Co.* [167 So. 595; cert. den. 167 So. 596]:

> At the common law an innkeeper, according to the prevailing, or majority view, was liable absolutely, as an insurer, "for all goods of a guest lost in the inn, unless the loss happens by an act of God, or a public enemy or by the fault or negligence of the guest himself." 32 C.J. 548,549 where the question is fully discussed.
>
> The "prevailing, or majority" view set out just next above is the one that obtains in Alabama. . . .
>
> The phrase "public enemy" is universally understood to mean some power with whom the government is at open war. It does not include robbers.

Thus the Alabama court held that robbers and thieves were not within the definition of public enemies, and the hotel was still liable for loss of the guest's property. This was a generally accepted proposition.

In a similar case arising many years later in Pennsylvania the court upheld the same common law liability of the hotel when a theft was involved while the victim was a guest in the hotel. In *Buck v. Hankin* [217 Pa.Super. 262, 269 A.2d 344 (1970)] the court stated:

> Also, the defense seems to imply that common law liability extends to a loss occurring when the guest is not in his room but does not extend to a forcible taking when the guest is in his room. With this view we cannot

agree. A guest is entitled to the protection of his goods which the common law affords him whether or not he is in the room at the time the goods are stolen . . .

Often a guest will check valuables with the front desk for safe keeping. Is the hotel liable for the loss when armed robbers steal the property? In a case arising in Minnesota the guest had her son take two diamond rings belonging to her and check them with the hotel clerk. A claim ticket with a number corresponding to the number of an envelope in which the rings were placed was given to the son. The envelope was placed in the hotel safe located in the front office a few feet behind the reception desk. Though equipped with a combination lock, the safe had not been locked for many years. A clerk was, however, always on duty at the desk. During the night two armed men robbed the hotel, taking the rings. When the guest sued the hotel for the value of the rings the hotel defended by claiming that the robbery relieved it of liability for the loss. In holding the hotel responsible the court found a bailment relationship to have been created and the hotel negligent in failing to keep the safe locked at night. [See *Wallinga v. Johnson* 131 N.W.2d 216 (Minn. 1964).]

The fault of the guest himself in causing loss of property was recognized by the common law as relieving the hotel from liability. While the general principle is easy enough to state, applying the principle is not always so simple. Attempting to determine if actions of a guest are a sufficient causative factor in the loss can be rather difficult. In *Buck v. Hankin, supra,* the plaintiff was a paying guest at a motel. Plaintiff had retired for the evening, opening a window in his room. During the night a prowler pried open the screen over the window and entered the room, robbing the plaintiff of jewelry and money. Plaintiff filed suit against the motel to recover for loss of his belongings; in its defense the motel, among other things, alleged that the plaintiff was himself contributorily negligent in that he had opened the window through which the prowler entered. In its decision, however, the court did not hold that such action by the plaintiff constituted negligence contributing to his own loss and upheld the plaintiff's right to recover. The court did, however, again recognize the basic common law principle that a guest would not be able to recover for loss of property if the guest in fact had assumed risk of loss or theft by lack of due care with respect to protecting his own possessions.

STATUTORY LIABILITY

The prior discussion has centered on the common law liability of an innkeeper for loss of a guest's property. The burden and responsibility placed upon the innkeeper, as previously discussed, were heavy. The innkeeper became virtually a guarantor of the safety of the guest's belongings while at the inn, and very few occurrences would relieve liability. This was the rule of law that developed early, with the practical consideration of protecting innocent travelers from sometimes unscrupulous innkeepers in league with thieves.

Today the majority of states have enacted legislation that protects hotel and motel operators from the liability otherwise imposed upon them by the common law. These statutes vary, but the effect is basically to *limit* liability of innkeepers for loss of guests' property. The individual state statute must be consulted for specifics. Some will limit the extent of liability or provide for limited liability when directions for depositing valuables are posted. Probably the most general pattern requires the guest to deliver his valuables for safekeeping to the innkeeper, who will then place them in a safe. Even then statutes may limit the dollar liability of the hotel for loss and may not even require the hotel to accept property over a stated value.

All of these statutes limiting the liability of the innkeeper for loss of property are in derogation of the common law. As such, the hotelkeeper must *strictly comply* with the provisions of the statute if he is to avail himself of its protection. [*Buck v. Hankin, supra; Skyways Motor Lodge v. General Foods Corp.* 403 A.2d 722 (Del. 1979).] Otherwise the common law will apply. Compliance may very often involve posting notices required by the statute in conspicuous places and perhaps taking other measures to assure that the guest has reasonable notice of limitations of liability.

The necessity of the hotelkeeper to comply *meticulously* with the applicable statute so as to relieve himself of the common law liability cannot be overemphasized. A Delaware case involving theft of property from a guest's room is illustrative. Failure of the hotel to comply strictly with the statute involved resulted in it being held to the common law standard of liability. The plaintiff's employee checked into the motor lodge concerned and carried with him a box of airplane parts belonging to his employer, the plaintiff. At the bottom of the registration card was printed, in small type: "Money, Jewels and Valuables Must Be Deposited In The Office Safe Otherwise The Proprietor Will Not Be Responsible For Any Loss." Because of the fine print the employee did not notice the statement and took the box of airplane parts to his room. The next morning after a brief absence the employee returned to his room to find the box of parts gone. At this time the employee noticed a sign posted on the back of his room door. The sign set forth room rates and in small type stated: "All moneys, jewelry, coats, valises, and other valuables must be left at the office and checks received therefore; otherwise the proprietor will not be responsible for any loss." The Delaware court on appeal upheld a judgment allowing the plaintiff to recover for the loss against the motor lodge for not strictly complying with the applicable statute. Thus an innkeeper's common law liability applied. In *Skyways Motor Lodge v. General Foods Corp.* [403 A.2d 722 (Del. 1979)] the court stated:

> As 24 Del. C. § 1502 seeks to modify the common law, it will be strictly construed . . . It follows that, in order to gain the Statute's protection an innkeeper must comply meticulously with its requirements.
>
> In this case Skyways was in noncompliance in two ways:
>
> Section 1502 requires, inter alia, notice of the existence of a "secure safe or vault" in which valuables may be deposited. Since the notice on the guest's motel room door did not advise him of the existence of such safe or vault, there was failure to comply with that express provision of the Statute.
>
> Furthermore, Skyways failed to comply with the requirement of § 1502 that it post the requisite notices "in every lodging room and other conspicuous places." It is undisputed that the required notice appeared only on the guest registration card and the room door, that therefore, the defendant failed to comply with the Statute's requirement.
>
> We hold, therefore, that Skyways was not entitled to the Statute's protection against an innkeeper's absolute liability at common law for the loss of the chattels of his guest.

Some statutes will under certain circumstances limit the hotel's liability for loss of articles entrusted to it to a fixed dollar amount but also provide for allowing the hotel, if it chooses, to agree to assume responsibility for a greater amount. Such was the case concerning an Oklahoma statute in the case of *Kalpakian v. Oklahoma Sheraton Corporation* [398 F.2d 243 (C.A. 10 1968)]. In *Kalpakian* the appellate court upheld the trial court's ruling that the hotel's liability was in that situation limited to $1500.00 Relevant portions of the case are presented hereafter: the relevant section of the Oklahoma statute is found in Appendix B of this book for the reader's reference.

> While on a selling trip, Edward Kalpakian, who with his wife Lucy is engaged in the wholesale and retail jewelry business, registered at the Sheraton in Oklahoma City on the evening of September 25, 1962.[2] He immediately requested a deposit box in the hotel vault in which to deposit his jewelry. Apparently he informed the hotel employee at the cashier's cage that he had "valuables" he wished to protect. The hotel maintained several sizes of deposit boxes, and at that hour no box of sufficient size to hold the case containing Kalpakian's jewelry was available.[3] It was necessary, therefore, to use a smaller box, which entailed removing the chamois rolls containing the jewelry from the bag prior to placing them in the safety deposit box. The following morning a larger box became available, and after removing his jewelry from the smaller box, he reserved the larger box for use later that day. A different employee was on duty at that time, and upon request Kalpakian signed a printed form then used by the hotel in connection with its safety deposit service. The form was designated "Oklahoma Biltmore Hotel Safe Deposit Box Agreement." In addition to stating that safety deposit boxes were available for hotel guests and referring to the return of the key, the instrument contained the following statement: "The maximum value of the property deposited shall not exceed $1500.00." The boxes could be opened only by the joint use of the hotel's master key and the key to the particular box issued to the guest. When Kalpakian returned later in the day, this procedure was followed and the case containing the jewelry was deposited. After the box was locked, Kalpakian retained his key. Upon opening the box the next morning, the case and jewelry had been removed and have not been subsequently found. It appears from the record that during the night a person other than Kalpakian appeared at the clerk's desk with a key to Kalpakian's box and requested entrance thereto, which was granted by the clerk.
>
> The prevailing view at common law was that an innkeeper was liable as an insurer for the property lost by a person while a guest in the inn. 43 C.J.S. Innkeepers § 15. This view was reflected in the Oklahoma Statutes, 1890, § 2752, (see Busby Hotel & Theatre Co. V. Thom, 125 Okl. 239, 257 P. 314), and in the same year the Oklahoma legislature provided a means by which an innkeeper might limit his liability by providing a safe for the valuables of his guests.[4] Implicit in the opinions of the Oklahoma Supreme Court construing this first statutory modification of the common law rule was the view that even though the hotel complied with the provisions of the statute, it would remain liable to guests for the negligent loss of their property. Ketchum v. Gordon, 151 Okl. 240, 298 P. 605; Huckins Hotel Co. v. Hooper, 44 Okl. 307, 144 P.

177. Following these decisions, the statutes under consideration here were enacted in 1939 significantly changing the liability of a hotel for the loss of a guest's property.

15 Okl.St.Ann. §§ 501, 503, 503a and 503b fix the liability of the operator, manager or owner of a hotel in Oklahoma for loss of personal property belonging to guests. Section 503 makes it the duty of the hotel to equip the doors of all guest rooms with suitable night latches, night chains or bolts, placed on the inside of the doors to prevent opening from the outside by key or otherwise. Section 503a[5] relates to hotels which provide a safe, vault or other depository for the safekeeping of valuables described therein. Notice that such safe, vault or other depository is available to guests shall be given by posting a notice in a public and conspicuous place and manner in the office or public rooms, or in the parlors or guest rooms of the hotel. The statute provides that if after notice, a hotel guest neglects to deposit valuables in the hotel depository, the hotel shall not be liable for any loss of property belonging to a guest, regardless of the cause. But when valuables are delivered for deposit, the statute requires that the guest shall at that time advise the person in charge of the hotel office of the actual value of the property, and the hotel is not required to accept property for deposit exceeding the value of $300. If there is a loss of deposited property, the hotel is liable only for the actual value thereof "in no event exceeding the sum of Three Hundred Dollars ($300.00)." The hotel, however, may by special agreement in writing with a guest, receive property of greater value than $300 and assume liability as shall be provided for in the written agreement.

The manifest purpose of Section 503a is to protect a hotel against undisclosed excessive liability when it furnishes for its guests safety deposit facilities, and to provide a method for accepting greater liability by written agreement if the hotel management desires. The decision to accept greater responsibility can be made only after the hotel guest has notified the hotel of the actual value of the deposited property. The statutory duty to give the notice of value is upon the guest. When the hotel knows the value of the property to be deposited, it may then determine whether it desires to accept the deposit and assume responsibility for its loss. Until the notice of value is given there is no liability for loss of the property beyond the $300.00 limit, regardless of the cause of the loss. As we said in Solomon v. Downtowner of Tulsa, Inc. with reference to a similar notice provision in Section 503b, "Under the Oklahoma Statute, the limitation of liability for loss of merchandise samples depends * * * upon the giving of the required notice by the guest." 357 F.2d 449, 451. The trend of the decisions considering state statutes relating to a hotel's liability for lost property deposited with it, is to strictly construe the obligation of a hotel guest to disclose the value of deposited property and to refuse to impose on hotels without notice a greater liability than the statutory amount, regardless of negligence. Oppenheimer v. Morton Hotel

Corp., W.D.Mich., 210 F.Supp. 609, aff'd 6 Cir., 324 F.2d 766; K. S. K. Jewelry Co. v. Chicago Sheraton Corp., 7 Cir., 283 F.2d 8; Lazare Kaplan & Sons, Inc. v. Pensacola Hotel Co., N.D.Fla., 153 F. Supp. 31, aff'd 5 Cir., 253 F.2d 410; David Karp Co. v. Read House, Inc., 6 Cir., 228 F.2d 185; Chase Rand Corp. v. Pick Hotels Corp. of Youngstown, 167 Ohio St. 299, 147 N.E.2d 849. The practice of pleading tort or negligence to avoid the restriction on liability was rejected in Eichberg & Co. v. Van Orman Fort Wayne Corp., 7 Cir., 248 F.2d 758, cert. denied 356 U.S. 927, 78 S.Ct. 716, 2L.Ed.2d 759, and Ricketts v. Morehead Co., 122 Cal.App.2d 948, 265 P.2d 963. Kalpakian argues that the statutory provisions do not relieve the hotel from liability for loss of deposited articles if caused by negligence whatever their value. To accept this construction would permit a guest to accomplish by non-disclosure what he could not accomplish by giving notice of value.

Kalpakian, when he requested a safety deposit box for his valuables, admittedly did not advise the person in charge of the hotel as to the actual value of the property. He signed an instrument submitted by the hotel which stated that the value of his property did not exceed $1500.00, and there is no evidence that the clerk who accepted the deposit knew that the value of the jewelry was greater than that amount. This instrument amounts to a notice upon which the hotel could rely in concluding whether it would accept liability for the deposited articles and limits recovery to $1500.00 in case of loss for any reason, including negligence.

The remaining contentions that the written notice of value was void, and that there was an issue of fact as to the sufficiency of the posted notice in the hotel are without merit. Although the signed instrument was labeled "Oklahoma Biltmore Safe Deposit Box Agreement", it was in fact used by Oklahoma Sheraton, and Kalpakian, to fix the deposit necessary to obtain a box from the Sheraton — not the Oklahoma Biltmore — and to establish the maximum value of the property deposited. Upon signing the instrument, Kalpakian was assigned and used a box which he knew was the property of Oklahoma Sheraton.

The purpose of the statutory requirement that notice of the availability of safety deposit boxes be posted in a conspicuous place is to limit liability of the hotel when there are losses by guests who do not deposit their valuables. Kalpakian had been a guest at the Sheraton on previous occasions. He knew that the safety deposit box facilities were available. He not only used them, but also signed an instrument acknowledging that the value of the property being deposited did not exceed $1500.00. Although the record indicates that the posted notices satisfied the statute, Kalpakian had actual notice and cannot complain of lack of the statutory constructive notice. Continental Supply Co. v. Marshall, D.C.Okl., 52 F.Supp. 717, rev'd on other grounds, 10 Cir., 152 F.2d 300, cert. denied 327 U.S. 803, 66 S.Ct. 962, 90 L.Ed. 1028.

The hotel's liability being limited to $1500.00, the court did not err in dismissing the action for lack of jurisdiction. City of Boulder v. Snyder, 10 Cir., 396 F.2d 853.

Affirmed.

Under the common law a hotel was liable for loss of a guest's effects even if caused by a robbery while the guest was at the hotel. [See *Johnston v. Mobile Hotel Co., supra.*] Statutes may modify this liability. In a Florida case [*de Saric v. Miami Caribe Investments Inc.* 512 F.2d 1013 (5th Cir. 1975)] a guest and her daughter had checked into their room. When ready to leave the room they were confronted by two armed men who robbed them of jewelry. There was in effect a statute limiting the liability of hotels to valuables deposited with the hotel. The guest had not deposited her valuables but had them with her in the room when stolen. Important portions of the case are presented here:

At common law, innkeepers were insurers of the property of their guests, and their liability was like that of a bailee. Since the innkeeper was being compensated for his services, he was a *bailee for hire* and thus subject to the standard of ordinary care. Adelphia Hotel Company v. Providence Stock Company, 3 Cir., 1922, 277 F. 905; Walpert v. Bohan, 126 Ga. 532, 55 S.E. 181 (1906). Many jurisdictions, including Florida, have limited an innkeeper's liability by statute. Enacted, as they were, in derrogation of the common law, these statutes have been strictly construed. Thompson v. Thompson 218 U.S. 611, 31 S.Ct. 111, 54 L.Ed. 1180 (1910); Johnston v. Mobile Hotel Company, 27 Ala.App. 145, 167 So. 595 (1936), cert, denied, 232 Ala. 175, 167 So. 596; 73 Am.Jur.2d, Statutes, § 287; 40 Am.Jur.2d, Hotels, Motels, etc., § 153 (1968).

In its decision, the District Court apparently relied on Ely v. Charellen Corporation, 5 Cir., 1941, 120 F.2d 984. As it develops, this case is the last word in this Court or from the Florida Courts dealing with the issue which, thirty-four years later, now makes its second appearance.

In *Ely,* the plaintiff registered at a Florida hotel. Jewelry was stolen from her room. At that time, as today, Florida law provided that a hotel was not liable for the loss of valuables unless deposited with the hotel management [Chapter 16042 Florida Acts, § 40 (1933), the forerunner of the present § 509.111]. Also in effect at that time, as today, was a requirement that the hotel post notice of this and other rules, Chapter 16042 Florida Act, § 38 (1933). In *Ely,* as in the case *sub judice,* neither party complied with the statutes, in that the plaintiff left valuables in her room and the hotel had failed to post notice of its liability limitations.

The plaintiff argued that the hotel's obligation to post notice of the

Act had to be met before the hotel could claim its benefits. This Court, in a one page opinion, held that because § 40 listed no exceptions, no liability would attach to the hotel proprietor for the loss of jewelry unless it was deposited with the hotel. We noted that § 40 provided that *in no event* would a hotel be liable for loss of goods not deposited with the hotel (emphasis ours). This same "in no event" language appears in the present statute. The statutes have been amended by the Florida legislature three times since *Ely,* always retaining the "in no event" phraseology which *Ely* held to be decisive regardless of whether the statutory notice had, or had not been, posted.

The outstanding, unreversed decision in *Ely* is binding on us.

In their brief, appellants state their position on this point as follows:

> "As the plaintiffs had not yet deposited their valuables with the management at the time of the robbery, we have stipulated that if the statute applies to the facts of this case, and is constitutional, then the plaintiffs are barred from recovering for their loss of personal property. If, on the other hand, the statute does not apply, or is unconstitutional, then the defendants are strictly liable for plaintiff's loss of personal property."

We are of the opinion that the statute does apply because it refers to *any loss,* which could apply to losses by robbery as well as from any other source. Accordingly, we cannot accept the argument that the statute applies only to items which guests have carelessly left in their rooms, subject to the possibility of theft.

In each state the statutory law must be consulted to see what limitations are in effect with respect to liability for loss of a guest's property. There is variation in the law on this point as previously noted. Hotelkeepers must be certain that they strictly comply with statutory requirements to avail themselves of limited liability. In Florida the statutes, as is typical, require posting of notice to guests. The law concerning liability for guests' property is found in Florida Statute § 509.111:

(1) The operator of a public lodging establishment is under no obligation to accept for safekeeping any moneys, securities, jewelry, or precious stones of any kind belonging to any guest, and, if such are accepted for safekeeping, he shall not be liable for the loss thereof unless such loss was the proximate result of fault or negligence of the operator. However, the liability of the operator shall be limited to $1,000 for such loss, if the public lodging establishment gave a receipt for the property (stating the value) on a form which stated, in type large enough to be clearly noticeable, that the public lodging establishment was not liable for any loss exceeding $1,000 and was only liable for that amount if the

loss was the proximate result of fault or negligence of the operator.

(2) The operator of a public lodging establishment shall not be liable or responsible to any guest for the loss of wearing apparel, goods, or other property, except as provided in subsection (1), unless such loss occurred as the proximate result of fault or negligence of such operator, and, in case of fault or negligence, he shall not be liable for a greater sum than $500, unless the guest, prior to the loss or damage, files with the operator an inventory of his effects and the value thereof and the operator is given the opportunity to inspect such effects and check them against such inventory. The operator of a public lodging establishment shall not be liable or responsible to any guest for the loss of effects listed in such inventory in a total amount exceeding $1,000.

As previously illustrated in this chapter the courts tend to require that the hotel operator very strictly comply with statutes limiting the hotel's liability for loss of guests' property; failure to do so usually results in a loss by the hotel of the benefit of the limitation of liability. In *Zacharia v. Harbor Island Spa Inc.* [684 F.2d 199 (2nd Cir. 1982)] the plaintiff/guest was staying at defendant's hotel and had deposited certain jewelry with the hotel to be kept in the hotel's safety deposit boxes. Plaintiff signed two cards, said cards indicating that the hotel's liability was limited to $1000.00 for loss of property. The hotel did not, however, give to plaintiff any receipt or a copy of the card containing the limitation as required by the state statute in force. When plaintiff's jewelry was lost, due to a theft, she was allowed, on appeal, to pursue a recovery in excess of $1000.00 for the loss. In holding the statutory limit on liability inapplicable under the circumstances the court wrote:

Section 509.111(1) provides that a hotel's liability may be limited only if the hotel "gave a receipt for the property (stating the value)." Plaintiff was given no document of any kind in connection with use of the safe deposit box. All of the documentation was retained by the Hotel in accord with its established practices. . . . We can only speculate as to the result a Florida court would reach on these facts. Relevant Florida decisions, however, emphasize that the burden of compliance is on the hotel rather than on the guest, since the hotel has "superior position and knowledge . . . with regard to the mandates of the statute," . . . We hold that the Hotel's casual attitude toward even the plainest requirement of the statute deprives it of the benefit of the limitation of liability. There is no ambiguity as to the statute's requiring that a document constituting a statutory receipt must be *given* to the guest depositing valuables. This receipt requirement is obviously designed to emphasize to the guest the

> statutory limitation since access to the valuables on each occasion is only by production of this document to Hotel officials. No document was given to Zacharia then or on any of the numerous occasions on which she entered the box. Although additional valuables might have been deposited at any time, the Hotel made no attempt to give direct notice to Zacharia of its purported limited liability except on the first deposit.

This case again well illustrates the need for hotels and motels to be careful that they comply with all provisions of state statutes that limit their liability for loss of a guest's property. As in the above example, any failure to comply *strictly* will often lead to loss of the statute's benefit.

The types of property for which loss a statute will limit liability are somewhat varied and subject to court interpretation as well. In the New York case of *Federal Ins. Co. v. Waldorf Astoria Hotel* [60 Misc.2d 996, 303 N.Y.S.2d 297 (1969)] the court, in interpreting a statute limiting a hotelkeeper's liability, ruled that gold cuff links ornamented with a pearl in each one could not be considered as "jewels" or "ornaments" within the meaning of the statute that absolved a hotelkeeper from liability for loss of "jewels, ornaments, or precious stones" not placed in a safe provided by the hotel.

In Appendix B are reprinted sections 200 and 201 of the New York General Business Law so the reader may have another statute to compare with the Florida statute respecting limiting liability. Similarities will be noted but also differences, such as dollar amount limitations. If the hotel does not comply with the applicable statutory law then the common law liability of innkeepers is imposed, and the hotel then virtually guarantees safety of property.

When a statute requires posting of notices with respect to limits of liability the hotel or motel should exercise great care to post such notices in such places as the law expressly demands. The form and contents of the notice should be carefully examined to ascertain that it satisfies statutory requirements. It might also be well expressly to inform guests checking in of the law in effect in the state. When the hotel has been careful in complying with the law it should then be able to rely on its protection. It would be beneficial for all those persons in the hospitality industry carefully to review the law in force in their particular state. Only then may they properly govern their actions.

CHAPTER 5

FOOD SERVICE LIABILITY

IN earlier years it was most common for an inn to make meals available to its guests lodging there. This was a substantial convenience to travelers in an era when places in which one could obtain a meal were relatively few and far between. Today, of course, all types of restaurants are in most parts of the country quite accessible to the traveler, from the very posh ones to the familiar fast-food stand. While it is not necessary for an establishment to maintain a restaurant operation on the premises to maintain the status of a hotel or motel, many do, in fact, offer some type of food service to guests and other patrons. Having a restaurant facility on the grounds is often a valuable asset to the business in attracting the traveler who is looking for such a convenience. Most often the facility is open to the general public as well as guests. It may be an integral part of the business, as a formal dining room in a hotel, or it may be a food service that is merely ancillary in nature, such as a small breakfast bar near a pool.

What is the liability when a food service operation provides a customer with food or drink that causes some illness or injury to the customer? There are various legal theories under which an injured party may seek to recover damages. One of these is negligence, the basic theory of which was discussed in an earlier chapter of this book. A restaurant owes a duty to its customers to exercise reasonable care in the preparation and serving of food and drink. If it fails to live up to this duty by failing to act as a reasonably prudent man would under the circumstances, and as a result injury is caused to a customer, then the restaurant will likely be found negligent and required to compensate the injured customer for damages sustained. Of course the acts of the restaurant must be shown to have been the proximate cause of the alleged injury for there to be a recovery. As a practical matter restaurants must exercise care in acquiring provisions, properly storing them, and properly preparing meals under sanitary conditions. To fail to use reasonable care and to act in a prudent manner may result in serious consequences for the business if a customer as a result is injured or becomes ill.

A case arising in Oregon is illustrative of the need to act with care in preparing food. A negligence action was brought against a restaurant by a plaintiff who contracted acute staphyloccal gastroenteritis after having eaten breakfast at the restaurant. The evidence indicated that the plaintiff ate only part of the food because it tasted rancid and had a slight odor, and medically the timing of the illness was appropriate compared to the plaintiff's ingestion of the food. The rancid taste and slight odor of the food were evidence from which a jury could infer that there was some outward manifestation of unwholesomeness of the food that one of the defendant restaurant's employees, exercising reasonable care, should have noticed. [*Gardyjan v. Tatone* 528 P.2d 1332.] Negligence may of course manifest itself in other ways aside from allowing spoiled food to be used in the preparation of a meal. Failure to exercise proper care in preparation, which results in the food becoming contaminated or foreign substances getting into it, may be actionable as well if it causes injury or illness to a customer.

Aside from the theory of negligence in the preparation and serving of food there are other legal concepts under which the provider of the food may be held responsible if the food is not wholesome. One of these is breach of warranty. In most jurisdictions when there is a *sale* of food or drink there is an implied warranty of fitness made by the seller to the purchaser. If it turns out that the food or drink is in fact unfit for consumption and injury is caused the purchaser, then the seller may be held liable to the purchaser for breach of warranty. This is so even where there is no negligence on the part of the seller. Breach of warranty liability is not based upon fault of the seller. Simply because a sale is made by one in the business, certain warranties may be implied under the law. It may be noted here that a lawsuit seeking damages could be based upon either a theory of negligence, breach of warranty, or both.

The question often arose in the past whether or not the furnishing of food and drink to hotel guests was in fact a "sale" of the food and drink so as to impose a warranty liability on the hotel or whether it was merely incidental to the service provided by the hotel. Two schools of thought developed. The so-called Connecticut – New Jersey rule held that no "sale" imposing liability under a warranty was involved. This view and the reasoning for it were set forth by the court in *Lynch v. Hotel Bond Co.* [117 Conn. 128, 167 A. 99 (1933)]:

> The business of a hotel or restaurant is not that of a dealer in commodities. The food in the ice box is not kept there for sale, but to be cooked, if required, and served to the guests of the establishment as ordered. The only thing that is "sold" is the personal service rendered in the preparation and presentation of the food, the various essentials to its comfortable consumption or other facilities provided, and the privilege of consuming so much of the meal ordered as the guest may desire. Service is the predominant feature of the transaction. . . . Regardless of whether or not the transaction is a sale, it is said that upon grounds of public policy courts should hold the innkeeper and the restaurant keeper to warrant the wholesomeness of the food which they serve, that his opportunity to discover and provide against deleterious food is as ample as is that of a retail dealer in food stuffs, and that he should be held to the same liability. We are not prepared to say that the protection of the public requires the imposition upon the innkeeper of absolute liability for the quality of the food served by him, contrary to the long-established rule that his obligation is limited to the exercise of due care in the preparation and service of the food furnished to his guests.

In contrast, the so-called Massachusetts – New York rule adopted by other courts maintained that such a furnishing of food and drink was a sale so as to impose warranty liability. This was the more modern trend. This view of the issue was illustrated well by a Florida case, *Cliett v. Lauderdale Biltmore Corporation* 39 So.2d 476 (1949)]. Relevant portions of the opinion of the court are presented here.

> SEBRING, Justice.
>
> The appellee, the proprietor of a hotel and dining room, served a meal containing unwholesome food to the appellant, a paying guest, who became ill as the result of its impurity. The appellant sued the proprietor for damages resulting from his illness, on the theory of an implied warranty that the food was fit for human consumption. A demurrer was sustained to the declaration with leave to plead over. The

appellant refused to amend his declaration, submitted to the entry of a final judgment in bar of the action, and prosecuted the present appeal from the final judgment.

The sole question for determination on the pleading is whether the proprietor of a public restaurant or dining room who serves a meal containing unwholesome food to a paying guest for immediate consumption on the premises is under an absolute liability for the damages proximately resulting from the impurities, on the theory of an implied warranty of fitness.

The question is one of first impression in this jurisdiction. In other states where the issue has been presented the courts have been in sharp division on the matter. Some courts have held that in the absence of statute a victualer serving food for immediate consumption on the premises may not be held liable for food deleterious to health, without proof that he was guilty of negligence; while others have determined that aside from any question of negligence, such a purveyor of foods for a valuable consideration is under an absolute liability for unwholesome food served by him, on the theory of an implied warranty of fitness. . . .

In our opinion the implied warranty theory of liability comports with the general trend of the better reasoned cases and is supported, on principle at least, by decisions from our own jurisdiction.

In Blanton v. Cudahy Packing Co., 154 Fla. 872, 19So.2d 313, this court held that a manufacturer and packer of tinned meat products was liable for injuries sustained by a buyer who became sick from eating the product which had been purchased in the original tin from a retail grocer, on the theory that the transaction involved a sale out of which there arose an implied warranty as between the manufacturer and the ultimate consumer that the food was wholesome and fit for human consumption. In Smith v. Burdine's Inc., 144 Fla. 500, 198 So. 223, 131 A.L.R. 115, it was decided that a retailer of lipstick which contained poisonous substances was liable for injuries sustained by the purchaser as the result of its use, on the theory that the transaction involved a sale out of which there arose an implied warranty as between the retailer and the purchaser that the article was harmless and not deleterious to health when properly used.

These cases establish the principle that as to items of foods or other products in the original package which are offered for sale for human consumption or use generally, a person who purchases such items in reliance upon the express or implied condition or assurance that they are wholesome and fit for the uses or purposes for which they are advertised or sold, and who is injured as the result of unwholesome or deleterious substances therein which are unknown to the buyer, may hold either the manufacturer or the retailer liable in damages for injuries sustained by him, on the theory of an implied warranty of wholesomeness or fitness of such article or product for the purposes for which it was offered to the public.

The appellee maintains that the principle of implied warranty established by the Florida cases has no bearing on the facts of the case at bar, for the reason that the purchase of a meal in a restaurant does not involve the "sale" of the items of food ordered but only the purchase of a "service" of which the food is but an incidental part, and hence that the doctrine of implied warranty is not applicable.

The contention advanced by the appellee is supported by some of the decisions from other jurisdictions. And, though we express no opinion on the point, the principle may have some application to meals served "boarding house style", where the guests have no voice in the selection of the items of food to be prepared for their use and no real ownership in the victuals placed before them but only the right to consume such as they need and take no more. But we cannot see its soundness where the transaction is with respect to a table d'hote meal or one by the a la carte method of choosing each item the guest desires. To say that when one selects his soup, entree, vegetables, dessert and beverage individually from a wide variety of items listed on a menu, only a "service," and not a "sale" of the meal purchased, is involved, and that because of that fact the restaurant keeper may escape liability for unwholesome or poisonous food served to a paying guest unless the latter can point to specific acts of negligence in its care or preparation, seems basically unsound. As pointed out in Vold on Sales, Sec. 153, p. 477: "Whatever may have been the case in the more remote past, the present day conditions under which meals are served on a commercial basis have served to blur any sharp outlines there may once have been between the facts of service of food at an inn or restaurant and the sale of food in a grocery store."

We can perceive no substantial basis for holding a restaurant keeper who serves food for immediate consumption on the premises to a less degree of responsibility than that imposed upon a retailer who sells food for immediate consumption off the premises. Whether such a transaction be termed a service or a sale every argument for implying a warranty in the ordinary sale of food over the grocery counter for consumption off the premises would seem to be applicable with as great a degree of force to the purchase of a meal for consumption in a hotel dining room or restaurant. "The basis of implied warranty is justifiable reliance on the judgment or skill of the warrantor, and to charge the seller of an unopened can of food for the consequences of the inferiority of the contents of the can, and to hold free from liability a restaurant-keeper who opens the can on his premises and serves its contents to a customer, would be a strange inconsistency." Cushing v. Rodman, 65 App.D.C. 258, 82 F.2d 864, 868, 104 A.L.R. 1023.

Indeed, it would seem that if any distinction were to be drawn between the retailer and the restaurant keeper in such a transaction, the duty of the latter should be greater than that of the retailer who in many instances has no better opportunity for knowledge of the fact that certain foods may contain deleterious substances than has the ultimate consumer who purchases the article. For in a sense the restaurant keeper is the direct manufacturer of the meals he prepares in his own kitchen and serves to his guests in his dining room. It is hardly possible to think of any dishes prepared by him wherein his opportunity for knowledge of the ingredients is not far greater than that of the customer, hence he is in a position largely, if not entirely, denied to the guest to judge of their fitness before he serves them. As between the paying guest, who has no real means of determining whether the meal served is fit for human consumption, and the restauranteur, who is in a position to determine this fact before and during the period of preparation, the burden should properly rest with the one who has or should have such facilities to keep the food pure and fresh as to make an injury to the customer from their use highly improbable if not impossible.

We hold, therefore, that with respect to the guest of a hotel dining room or restaurant who receives, eats and pays for victuals delivered to him on his order, the proprietor must be held to the same degree of duty as regards the wholesomeness of such food as the law imposes upon a retailer of foods and other like products for consumption away from the premises.

From the conclusions reached, it follows that the declaration in the case at bar stated a cause of action for the recovery of damages to the appellant through being made ill on account of the unwholesomeness of the food ordered and consumed in the dining room of the appellee, on the theory of an implied warranty of fitness of the food served him, and that consequently the demurrer to the declaration should have been overruled.

The judgment appealed from is reversed and the cause is remanded for further proceedings in accordance with law.

It is so ordered.

Essentially the same warranty liability was imposed upon a restaurant in a Louisiana case in *Arnaud's Restaurant Inc. v. Cotten* [212 F.2d 883 (C.A. 5 1954)], further showing a trend to accept this concept.

In an effort to unify the law in certain areas with respect to trade and commerce the Uniform Commercial Code was drafted some years ago. With slight changes it has been adopted by most states and made a part of their statutory law. While the drafters of the Code recognized that there was a split of authority among courts in the land whether the furnishing of food and drink was a "sale," as discussed above, in the official comments to section 2-314 of the Code the drafters rejected those cases holding the transaction not a sale.

Today, under section 2-314 of the Uniform Commercial Code the serving for value of food and drink is to be considered a sale. This section of the code, as adopted in Florida as Florida Statute 672.314 is as follows:

> (1) Unless excluded or modified (672.316), a warranty that the goods shall be merchantable is implied in a contract for their sale if the seller is a merchant with respect to goods of that kind. Under this section the serving for value of food or drink to be consumed either on the premises or elsewhere is a sale.
>
> (2) Goods to be merchantable must be at least such as:
>
> > (a) Pass without objection in the trade under the contract description; and
> >
> > (b) In the case of fungible goods, are of fair average quality within the description; and
> >
> > (c) Are fit for the ordinary purpose for which such goods are used; and
> >
> > (d) Run, within the variations permitted by the agreement, of even kind, quality and quantity within each unit and among all units involved; and
> >
> > (e) Are adequately contained, packaged, and labeled as the agreement may require; and
> >
> > (f) Conform to the promises or affirmations of fact made on the container or label if any.
>
> (3) Unless excluded or modified (672.316) other implied warranties may arise from course of dealing or usage of trade.

Today there is little question that the seller of food or drink under the law impliedly warrants that what is provided, is fit for consumption. Of course the term *seller,* as noted, is not limited to grocers or vendors but would encompass restaurants as well. Again, this liability of the seller is irrespective of any fault or negligence on the part of the seller. Frequently, though, questions as to *what* renders food or drink unfit for consumption so as to constitute a breach of implied warranty of fitness have arisen. Food that is spoiled is obviously unfit and if sold there would be liability on the seller.

In deciding *what* renders food unfit for consumption courts have approached the problem somewhat differently. When an injury is caused by a "foreign" substance found in the food, such as a piece of glass in a piece of pie, there is little question but what the injured customer may recover. A piece of pie with such a substance in it is certainly not fit to be consumed. More difficult problems arise when the substance causing the injury is "natural" such as a cherry pit in a piece of cherry pie. States following the "foreign versus natural" test would hold that if the substance is natural, with respect to the food in which it is found, then it does not render the food unfit so as to impose warranty liability upon the seller. Other states reject this position and follow the "reasonable expectation" test, that is, what is reasonable for the customer to expect in the *prepared* food as opposed to what is natural to it before preparation. Following is a case concerning whether or not a fish bone in a fish chowder rendered the chowder unfit [*Webster v. Blue Ship Tea Room, Inc.* 198 N.E.2d 309 (Mass. 1964)].

*REARDON, Justice.

This is a case which by its nature evokes earnest study not only of the law but also of the culinary traditions of the Commonwealth which bear so heavily upon its outcome. It is an action to recover damages for personal injuries sustained by reason of a breach of implied warranty of food served by the defendant in its restaurant. An auditor, whose findings of fact were not to be final, found for the plaintiff. On a retrial in the Superior Court before a judge and jury, in which the plaintiff testified, the jury returned a verdict for her. The defendant is here on exceptions to the refusal of the judge (1) to strike certain portions of the auditor's report, (2) to direct a verdict for the defendant, and (3) to allow the defendant's motion for the entry of a verdict in its favor under leave reserved.

The jury could have found the following facts: On Saturday, April 25, 1959, about 1 P. M., the plaintiff, accompanied by her sister and her aunt, entered the Blue Ship Tea Room operated by the defendant. The group was seated at a table and supplied with menus.

This restaurant, which the plaintiff characterized as "quaint," was located in Boston "on the third floor of an old building on T Wharf which overlooks the ocean."

The plaintiff, who had been born and brought up in New England (a fact of some consequence), ordered clam chowder and crabmeat salad. Within a few minutes she received tidings to the effect that "there was no more clam chowder," whereupon she ordered a cup of fish chowder. Presently, there was set before her "a small bowl of fish chowder." She had previously enjoyed a breakfast about 9 A. M. which had given her no difficulty. "The fish chowder contained haddock, potatoes, milk, water and seasoning. The chowder was milky in color and not clear. The haddock and potatoes were in chunks" (also a fact of consequence). "She agitated it a little with the spoon and observed that it was a fairly full bowl. . . . It was hot when she got it, but she did not tip it with her spoon because it was hot . . . but stirred it in an up and under motion. She denied that she did this because she was looking for something, but it was rather because she wanted an even distribution of fish and potatoes." She started to eat it, alternating between the chowder and crackers which were on the table with . . . [some] rolls. She ate about 3 or 4 spoonfuls then stopped. She looked at the spoonfuls as she was eating. She saw equal parts of liquid, potato and fish as she spooned it into her mouth. She did not see anything unusual about it. After 3 or 4 spoonfuls she was aware that something had lodged in her throat because she couldn't swallow and couldn't clear her throat by gulping and she could feel it." This misadventure led to two esophagoscopies at the Massachusetts General Hospital, in the second of which, on April 27, 1959, a fish bone was found and removed. The sequence of events produced injury to the plaintiff which was not insubstantial.

We must decide whether a fish bone lurking in a fish chowder, about the ingredients of which there is no other complaint, constitutes a breach of implied warranty under applicable provisions of the Uniform Commercial Code,[1], the annotations to which are not helpful on this point. As the judge put it in his charge, "Was the fish chowder fit to be eaten and wholesome? . . . [N]obody is claiming that the fish itself wasn't wholesome. . . . But the bone of contention here — I don't mean that for a pun — but was this fish bone a foreign substance that made the fish chowder unwholesome or not fit to be eaten?"

The plaintiff has vigorously reminded us of the high standards imposed by this court where the sale of food is involved (see Flynn v. First Natl. Stores Inc., 296 Mass. 521, 523, 6 N.E.2d 814) and has made reference to cases involving stones in beans (Friend v. Childs Dining Hall Co., 231 Mass. 65, 120 N.E. 407, 5 A.L.R. 1100), trichinae in pork (Holt v. Mann, 294 Mass. 21, 22, 200 N.E. 403), and to certain other cases, here and elsewhere, serving to bolster her contention of breach of warranty.

The defendant asserts that here was a native New Englander eating fish chowder in a "quaint" Boston dining place where she had been before; that "[f]ish chowder, as it is served and enjoyed by New Englanders, is a hearty dish, originally designed to satisfy the appetites of our seamen and fishermen"; that "[t]his court knows well that we are not talking of some insipid broth as is customarily served to convalescents." We are asked to rule in such fashion that no chef is forced "to reduce the pieces of fish in the chowder to miniscule size in an effort to ascertain if they contained any pieces of bone." "In so ruling," we are told (in the defendant's brief), "the court will not only uphold its reputation for legal knowledge and acumen, but will, as loyal sons of Massachusetts, save our world-renowned fish chowder from degenerating into an insipid broth containing the mere essence of its former stature as a culinary masterpiece." Notwithstanding these passionate entreaties we are bound to examine with detachment the nature of fish chowder and what might happen to it under varying interpretations of the Uniform Commercial Code.

Chowder is an ancient dish preëxisting even "the appetites of our seamen and fishermen." It was perhaps the common ancestor of the "more refined cream soups, purées, and bisques." Berolzheimer, The American Woman's Cook Book (Publisher's Guild Inc., New York, 1941) p. 176. The word "chowder" comes from the French "chaudière," meaning a "cauldron" or "pot." "In the fishing villages of Brittany . . . 'faire la chaudière' means to supply a cauldron in which is cooked a mess of fish and biscuit with some savoury condiments, a hodge-podge contributed by the fishermen themselves, each of whom in return receives his share of the prepared dish. The Breton fishermen probably carried the custom to Newfoundland, long famous for its chowder, whence it has spread to Nova Scotia, New Brunswick, and New England." A New English Dictionary (MacMillan and Co., 1893) p. 386. Our literature over the years abounds in references not only to the delights of chowder but also to its manufacture. A namesake of the plaintiff, Daniel Webster, had a recipe for fish chowder which has survived into a number of modern cookbooks[2] and in which the removal of fish bones is not mentioned at all. One old time recipe recited in the New English Dictionary study defines chowder as "A dish made of fresh fish (esp. cod) or clams, stewed with slices of pork or bacon, onions, and biscuit. 'Cider and champagne are sometimes added.' " Hawthorne, in The House of the Seven Gables (Allyn and Bacon, Boston, 1957) p. 8, speaks of "[a] codfish of sixty pounds, caught in the bay, [which] had been dissolved into the rich liquid of a chowder." A chowder variant, cod "Muddle," was made in Plymouth in the 1890s by taking "a three or four pound codfish, head added. Season with salt and pepper and boil in just enough water to keep from burning. When cooked, add milk and piece of butter."[3] The recitation of these ancient formulae suffices to indicate that in the construction of chowders in these parts in other years, worries about fish bones played no role whatsoever. This broad outlook on chowders has persisted in more modern cookbooks. "The chowder of today is much the same as the old chowder. . . ." The American Woman's Cook Book, supra, p. 176. The all embracing Fannie Farmer states in a portion of her recipe, fish chowder is made with a "fish skinned, but head and tail left on. Cut off head and tail and remove fish from backbone. Cut fish in 2-inch pieces and set aside. Put head, tail, and backbone broken in pieces, in stewpan; add 2 cups cold water and bring slowly to boiling point. . . ." The liquor thus produced from the bones is added to the balance of the chowder. Farmer, The Boston Cooking School Cook Book (Little Brown Co., 1937) p. 166.

Thus, we consider a dish which for many long years, if well made, has been made generally as outlined above. It is not too much to say that a person sitting down in New England to consume a good New England fish chowder embarks on a gustatory adventure which may entail the removal of some fish bones from his bowl as he proceeds. We are not inclined to tamper with age old recipes by any amendment reflecting the plaintiff's view of the effect of the Uniform Commercial Code upon them. We are aware of the heavy body of case law involving foreign substances in food, but we sense a strong distinction between them and those relative to unwholesomeness of the food itself, e.g., tainted mackerel (Smith v. Gerrish, 256 Mass. 183, 152 N.E. 318), and a fish bone in a fish chowder. Certain Massachusetts cooks might cavil at the ingredients contained in the chowder in this case in that it lacked the heartening lift of salt pork. In any event, we consider that the joys of life in New England include the ready availability of fresh fish chowder. We should be prepared to cope with the hazards of fish bones, the occasional presence of which in chowders is, it seems to us, to be anticipated, and which, in the light of a hallowed tradition, do not impair their fitness or merchantability. While we are bouyed up in this conclusion by Shapiro v. Hotel Statler Corp., 132 F.Supp. 891 (S.D.Cal.), in which the bone which afflicted the plaintiff appeared in "Hot Banquette of Seafood Mornay," we know that the United States District Court of Southern California, situated as are we upon a coast, might be expected to share our views. We are most impressed, however by Allen v. Grafton, 170 Ohio St. 249 164 N.E.2d 167, where in Ohio, the Midwest, in a case where the plaintiff was injured by a piece of oyster shell in an order of fried oysters, Mr. Justice Taft (now Chief Justice) in a majority opinion held that "the possible presence of a piece of oyster shell in or attached to an oyster is so well known to anyone who eats oysters that we can say as a matter of law that one who eats oysters can reasonably anticipate and guard against eating such a piece of shell. . . ." (P. 259 of 170 Ohio St., p. 174 of 164 N.E.2d.)

Thus, while we sympathize with the plaintiff who has suffered a peculiarly New England injury, the order must be

Exceptions sustained.

Judgment for the defendant.

Other cases may involve a "natural" substance in the food, but it may be held that it is not reasonable to find it in the prepared food, and so liability is imposed on the seller of the food. A New York case involved negligence and breach of warranty allegations by the plaintiff against a restaurant owner for injury to the plaintiff's tooth when she bit into a "nutted cheese" sandwich that contained a rather large piece of walnut shell. In allowing the plaintiff to recover the court ruled that under the "reasonable expectation" test the plaintiff could expect not to find the shell in the prepared sandwich, even though it was a "natural" substance. (*Stark v. Chock Full O' Nuts* 77 Misc,2d 553, 356 N.Y.S.2d 403.)

A Louisiana case involved a natural substance but one found in a *different* food. The plaintiff suffered serious personal injuries involving his throat from ingesting a piece of crab shell in pompano en papilotte in the defendant's restaurant. On appeal a judgment in favor of the plaintiff against the restaurant was upheld. The court recognized that in Louisiana a business serving food was liable to a customer if the food was unwholesome and caused injury to the customer. In this case what was allegedly found in the food, crab shell, was not normally to be expected in the dish in which it was found. The crab shell in this case was foreign to the dish it was in. (*Arnaud's Restaurant Inc. v. Cotton* 212 F.2d 883.) The court stated:

> The principle, contended for by the defendants, that a customer who eats meat dishes ought to anticipate the presence of bones which are natural to the type meat served and cannot hold the restaurant keeper liable for an injury occurring as a result of the presence of such bones, is supported by a number of authorities, but it is not applicable to the facts of this case. Those cases are based upon the proposition that a bone natural to the meat which is served is not a foreign substance to that particular dish. Since the defendants admit, and the evidence shows, that Arnaud's does not use crab meat in the preparation of pompano en papilotte, we agree with the plaintiff that the piece of crab shell contained in the dish served to him was a foreign substance. It will not do to categorize all sea foods usually served in restaurants as a common dish.
>
> No affirmative evidence was offered by the defendants to sustain their defense of contributory negligence and thus the only evidence contained in the record upon which the jury could have found that the plaintiff was negligent was the fact that he failed to detect the presence of the crab shell before he swallowed it. We are unwilling to hold that his failure to discover the crab shell contained in the pompano en papilotte, served as it was and containing a number of ingredients, established contributory negligence as a matter of law. The circumstances presented an issue of fact for determination by the jury under proper instruction by the court as were given in this case.

As the prior discussion has indicated, one purchasing a meal may normally rely upon an implied warranty by the seller that the food is fit to be eaten. What if the injured patron is not the one paying for the meal? Can he recover? In at least one case it has been held immaterial that the injured patron of the restaurant was not the one paying the bill. Such injured person would be considered a purchaser even though another in his party was paying the bill, and thus the food server's implied warranty of fitness for consumption ran to him as well. (*Conklin v. Hotel Waldorf Astoria Corp.* 5 Misc.2d 496, 161 N.Y.S.2d 205.)

The preparation of food should certainly be done with care and under sanitary conditions. Modern technology has also imposed certain other considerations upon food preparers. Where microwave ovens are in use it is wise to post a notice of that fact; such notice may be required by law so as to warn those persons with heart pacemakers. Failure to do so could pose problems if injury is caused a guest or a customer.

Establishments, particularly lounges, that serve alcoholic beverages must be aware of so-called dram shop acts if in effect in the state. Under these statutes the seller of alcoholic beverages who sells them to an intoxicated person may be held liable to a third person who is injured due to the drunkenness of the intoxicated person. [See *Mitchell v. The Shoals Inc.* 227 N.Y.S.2d 113 (1967).]

The injured person may be outside the lounge, or it might be another customer who is injured by the drunken patron. In *Reibolt v. Bedient* [562 P.2d 991 (Wash. App. 1977)] a tavern customer sued the tavern owner after the customer was attacked and injured by another drunken customer, alleging the owner knew of the drunken attacker's condition and did nothing. The appellate court upheld a verdict in favor of the plaintiff for $75,000.00.

This chapter has briefly explored some problem areas related to the service of food and drink by hotels, motels, and restaurants. It is not all-inclusive, but the necessity of exercising great care in the preparation and service of food and drink should have been made clear. Even when there is no fault on the part of the preparer, he or she may be faced with warranty liability. In those cases the hotel or restaurant serving the food causing injury may have an action and recourse against a food supplier and/or processor if the food was initially bad when received. This, however, will not relieve the hotel of potential warranty liability to the injured customer, but it may at least allow a recovery from a party primarily at fault.

CHAPTER 6

ACTS OF EMPLOYEES – VICARIOUS LIABILITY

THE daily business operations of a hotel or motel, like any other business, must usually be conducted through agents or employees. Most of the actual work in the world is necessarily performed by employees of businesses. In the case of a hotel or motel it is necessary to have personnel employed to operate the front desk, to clean and maintain rooms and premises in general, to maintain security, and often to prepare food and drink for guests, among other functions. In the course of performing their assigned duties these employees may engage in conduct or activity that causes injury to a guest or his property, or perhaps to some third person. In such a situation the employee may be held liable for the injury caused, but frequently the employing hotel or motel is *also* held liable to the injured guest. The facts of each individual case are extremely important in ascertaining where liability lies, but very often the employing hotel or motel is held *vicariously* liable.

The legal doctrine under which the employer is usually held liable for the acts of its employees that cause injury to third parties is *respondeat superior* (literally, "let the master answer"). It is a common law maxim resting on the premise that there is a duty on the part of every person in handling his or her affairs and business, whether through agents or him/herself, to do so in such a manner as not to injure others. In *Mitchell v. Resto* [253 A.2d 25 (Conn. 1968)] the court stated: "Every man who prefers to manage his affairs through others remains bound to so manage them that third persons are not injured by any breach of legal duty on part of such others while they are engaged upon his business and within scope of their authority." Over the years various reasons and rationales have been proposed by the courts and other parties as to why the employer should be held legally liable for most acts of his or her employees that cause injury to third persons. One view held that the employer was in a position to exercise direction and control over the employee and thus should be responsible for his or her employees' acts. Another rationale for holding the employer liable is simply that the employer is usually thought to be better able to pay damages to an injured party than the employee. Other courts simply allocate the risk in this manner. In *Hinman v. Westinghouse Electric Company* [471 P.2d 988 (Cal. 1970)] the California court reviewed various concepts in its opinion:

> Although earlier authorities sought to justify the respondeat superior doctrine on such theories as "control" by the master of the servant, the master's "privilege" in being permitted to employ another, the third party's innocence in comparison to the master's selection of the servant, or the master's "deep pocket" to pay for the loss, the modern justification for vicarious liability is a rule of policy, a deliberate allocation of a risk. . . . The losses caused by the torts of employees, which as a practical matter are sure to occur in the conduct of the employer's enterprise, are placed upon the enterprise itself, as a required cost of doing business. They are placed upon the employer because, having engaged in an enterprise which will, on the basis of past experience, involve harm to others through the torts of employees, and sought to profit by it, it is just that he, rather than the innocent injured plaintiff, should bear them; and because he is better able to absorb them, and to distribute them, through prices, rates or liability insurance, to the public, and so to shift them to society, to the community at large. (Prosser, *Law of Torts* 3ed 1964.)

Generally if the employer is to be made to respond in damages for injuries sustained by third persons as the result of an employee's conduct it must be established that the employee's conduct was within the scope of his or her employment. For the employer to be held liable under *respondeat superior* the employee must have been acting to further the employer's interest when the injury occurred to the third person. Usually this poses no problem when the employee is engaged in his usual daily work and causes an injury as a result of his negligence. The employer, then, is usually held vicariously liable for the injury. An example might be where an employee has been engaged in washing and waxing the employer's floor and negligently allows a puddle of water to remain on the floor, causing a customer to slip and fall. Under the doctrine of respondeat superior the *employer* is held vicariously liable for the negligence of his or her employee. It should not matter that the employer has specifically instructed the employee not to allow any water to remain on the floor after the work is completed. If the employee has failed to heed such instructions and carelessly does allow such slippery substance to remain on the floor then this negligence on his or her part is still normally attributed to the employer. This should indicate that the employer should be careful to ascertain whether or not his employees are in fact following their instructions and orders properly. The argument may be made that this puts an unfair burden upon the employer, but if the employer was not held responsible then the innocent injured party would be required to bear the loss, and this would be a more unjust result.

Specifically what conduct of the employee is "within the scope of employment" is not always easy to determine especially if the conduct is unusual or not connected with ordinary duties. A great number of cases have been concerned with this issue, and it is not possible to set down herein any absolute guidelines. If an act of the employee has no relation to the employee's duties and if the act is engaged in only to further the employee's own personal interests, then it is likely that any injury caused will not be attributed to the employer. The facts of each case and the relationship between the conduct and the employment must be examined. Often the employee's motive in engaging in the conduct may be very important, as where it is not approved conduct but it is done with the intent on the part of the employee of attempting to benefit the employer. Where the acts of the employee are of a type and nature such as would be expected in the job performance, then such acts are normally within the scope of the employment. Sometimes even unusual acts, if foreseeable by the employer, are considered within the scope of employment. The employer in those cases is held liable for the results of such acts because it was within his contemplation that his or her employee might in fact engage in the conduct.

Some guidance in ascertaining whether conduct is within the scope of employment is found in section 228 of the Restatement of the Law, Agency 2d:

1. Conduct of a servant is within the scope of employment if, but only if:

    a. It is of the kind he is employed to perform,
    b. It occurs substantially within the authorized time and space limits,
    c. It is actuated, at least in part, by a purpose to serve the master, and
    d. If force is intentionally used by the servant against another, the use of force is not unexpectable by the master.

2. Conduct of a servant is not within the scope of employment if it is different in kind from that authorized, far beyond the authorized time or space limits, or too little actuated by a purpose to serve the master.

Further guidelines are discussed in section 229 of the Restatement, which is reproduced in Appendix C for the reader's reference. The nature of the conduct, whether or not it is commonly engaged in by similar employees, the prior relationship of employer and employee are all important considerations in the determination. It cannot be overemphasized that the factual setting of each individual situation is often crucial; each case is unique, and a slight change in facts could often lead to a very different outcome.

When an employee is engaged in performing his usual duties then his conduct is within the scope of employment so as to render the employer vicariously liable under the doctrine of respondeat superior. These cases usually do not pose great difficulties. Problems arise, however, where the conduct is unusual or unauthorized. Many of these cases have involved assaults by employees upon customers of the business establishment. In such a case is the employer to be held liable to the injured customer or patron? *Columbia By The Sea Inc. v. Petty* [157 So.2d 190 (Fla. App. 1963)] involved such a question. It was a suit against a restaurant owner and its maître d', where the plaintiff sought to recover damages for injuries he allegedly sustained as the result of an assault by the maître d'. A dispute had arisen over the bill for a meal that plaintiff had ordered, and this dispute supposedly culminated with the maître d' striking the plaintiff in the head with an ash tray. In considering the question of whether the assault was within the scope of employment of the maître d', so as to hold the employer liable, the court noted that the nature of the employee's duties and his motivation in acting, among other things, are to be considered, with each case involving the doctrine of respondeat superior being determined on its own unique facts.

It has long been recognized that a hotelkeeper has a duty to protect his guests from injury when he can do so by acting in a prudent manner. This would of course apply to injuries caused by acts of his own employees. An early case arising in Kentucky noted this. In *Ledington v. Williams* [78 S.W.2d 790 (Ky. App. 1935)] the court stated:

> However, the hotel keeper, it may be conceded, is alike under either rule under obligation to protect his guests from danger, when it is reasonably within his power to do so, and is also under an implied duty and obligation to knowingly select only such employees as are fit and suitable to look after the safety and comfort of his guests and who will not commit acts of violence against them, so far as is reasonably within his power to so choose and employ them.

Often an employee may use force against a customer or guest, and as a result an injury occurs and the employer is held liable. If use of force is part of the employee's duties or if it is at least foreseeable to the employer, then the employer may be held liable for resulting injuries to others. Cases such as this have frequently involved house detectives, "bouncers," or others employed for security and to keep order on the business premises. Even an ordinary employee may have the responsibility of keeping order in the business establishment. In *Anderson v. Covert* (193 Tenn. 238, 245 S.W.2d 770), the night man operating a restaurant evicted a disorderly patron using more force than was necessary. The employer in that case was held liable since the eviction was made by the employee as part of his employment; that the employee had lost his temper and used more force than necessary was not there controlling.

A case arising in Georgia involved allegations that a night desk clerk made an unprovoked attack upon and beat a guest. In that case the plaintiff/guest alleged after he and his wife had registered at the hotel operated by defendant they went to their room but had an argument. The wife left and went to another hotel for the night. Later, plaintiff became concerned that the wife might not have any money, and so at about 5 o'clock in the morning the plaintiff approached the desk clerk of his hotel, asking him to establish a credit for his wife at the other hotel. Plaintiff offered money to the clerk for the credit to be established, but the clerk informed the plaintiff that there was no connection with the plaintiff's hotel and the other hotel. The clerk then advised the plaintiff to go to the other hotel himself to make such arrangements for a credit. Plaintiff insisted that the credit could be arranged by the clerk, but the clerk disagreed. The plaintiff claimed that subsequently the clerk attacked and beat plaintiff with a blackjack. The clerk, conversely, alleged that when informed that the credit with the other hotel could not be arranged the plaintiff cursed him and reached for him and only then did the clerk hit the plaintiff. The court stated as follows in its opinion in the case of *Newton v. Candace Inc.* [94 S.E.2d 739 (Ga. App. 1956)]:

> 1. Like other masters, a hotel proprietor or innkeeper is liable for the torts of his servant committed in the performance of the duties the servant is employed to discharge and that could be reasonably expected of him in the prosecution of the proprietor's business.
>
> 2. It is the duty of an innkeeper not only to furnish his guest or patron with shelter and comforts but also to exercise ordinary care to protect him from danger. 28 Am. Jur., Innkeepers, § 52.
>
> 3. Hotels customarily transact business with patrons through the medium of clerks. It is within the scope of a hotel clerk's employment, when representing the proprietor of the establishment, to courteously reply to polite requests of the patron for accommodations of a lawful and moral nature irrespective of whether he or the hostelry is under any duty or can reasonably be expected to grant such requests. For a similar holding, though not precisely adjusted to the facts of this case, see Crawford v. Exposition Cotton Mills, 63 Ga. App. 458, 11 S.E.2d 234.
>
> 4. Where, as in the instant case, there was a conflict in the evidence, but some evidence supporting the contention of the plaintiff patron, that, when he tendered the necessary money for the purpose and politely requested of the defendant hotel proprietor's clerk that he arrange credit for his wife at another hotel, the clerk without provocation committed a violent assault upon him, thereby personally injuring and humiliating him, it was error, we grant a nonsuit on the assumption that the clerk when making the attack was not acting within the scope of his employment.

Thus the appeals court held that the trial court had made an error when the court itself dismissed the case on the basis that it held the clerk was not acting within the scope of his employment. Normally this may be a question for the jury, rather than the court, to decide upon the facts of the particular situation.

Sometimes a case will arise in which the facts appear to be that the employee made an assault or attack upon a guest for purely personal reasons, unrelated to furthering the interests of his employer or performing his duties as an employee. If the employee loses his temper and attacks a guest for purely personal reasons, and the employer cannot be charged with any knowledge of the employee's potentially dangerous propensities, and the employee is truly acting on his own without thought for his employer's benefit, then the employer should not normally be held responsible for the employee's acts, under the doctrine of respondeat superior. The doctrine is not applied in such a manner that the business is held responsible for totally personal acts of the employee in such a case. The New York case of *Moritz v. Pines Hotel Inc.* [383 N.Y.S.2d 704 (1976)] is illustrative of this idea. The assault in this case appeared totally outside the scope of the employee's duties and not in any sense engaged in to further any interest of the employing hotel.

> Appeal from a judgment of the Supreme Court in favor of defendants, entered August 14, 1975 in Sullivan County, upon a decision of the court at a Trial Term, without a jury, dismissing plaintiffs' complaint.
>
> The facts are not in dispute. Mrs. Moritz and Miss Ellison were paying guests at defendants' hotel in Sullivan County. After attending a lecture on the use of fabrics the two ladies were seated on a setee in the upper lobby of the hotel when a hotel porter, William Brown, dropped a heavy commercial vacuum cleaner on the knee of Miss Ellison. When the ladies complained, he verbally abused them and struck Mrs. Moritz forcibly in the face with his fist, knocking her over the setee, rendering her unconscious, and causing her to sustain painful and serious injuries.
>
> Upon this record the factual findings of the trial court that the assault was not done in furtherance of the defendants' business and thus not within the scope of employment cannot be disturbed. William Brown, the porter, was hired by defendants to perform menial tasks having to do with cleaning the public rooms of defendants' premises and the discharge of those duties in no way entailed the exercise of judgment and discretion, nor were such duties related to the maintaining of order in the hotel (*De Wolf v. Ford,* 193 N.Y. 397, 86 N.E. 527). An act is within the scope of a servant's employment when it is necessary to accomplish the purpose of his employment and intended for that purpose. An employee acts in the scope of his employment when he is doing something in furtherance of the duties he owes his employer and when the employer is, or could be, exercising some control directly or indirectly over the employee's activities (*Lundberg v. State,* 25 N.Y.2d 467, 306 N.Y.S.2d 947, 255 N.E.2d 177). The act of the employee for which

> the employer is sought to be held liable may not be outside the general scope of the employment or done with a purpose foreign to the interests of the employer (*Sauter v. New York Tribune, Inc.*, 305 N.Y. 442, 444, 113 N.E.2d 790, 791). Herein, the assault was not necessary or even incidental to the duties of the employee and was an act that could not have been foreseen or controlled by defendants. Next, it cannot be said that the assault was not foreign to the interests of the defendants. The assault was a sudden, inexplicable act without apparent purpose and completely outside the duties and scope of the assailant's employment and is not chargeable to the employer under the doctrine of *respondeat superior.*

Just as in the case where an employee assaults a guest for personal reasons, if an employee commits a criminal act against a guest it will probably be considered definitely beyond the scope of employment. A hotel or motel certainly does not hire one to commit crimes against its guests, and thus will not usually be held responsible under the doctrine of respondeat superior. The hotel or motel may, however, have been negligent in hiring or retaining the employee in question. When a business hires a person whom it knows has dangerous propensities (perhaps a history of assaults on others) and places that person in a position of employment where there is much exposure to the public, then the employer may be negligent in so doing. With respect to criminal acts of employees as mentioned previously it is well to look at part of the court's opinion in *Harvey v. DeWeil* [116 S.E.2d 747 (Ga. App. 1960)] wherein the case involved the claim that an employee attacked a guest:

> It is elementary and requires no citation of authority that when an employee of a motel enters the room of a guest for the purpose of committing larceny or felonious assault upon the guest, the employee has departed from the scope of his employment and is engaged upon a frolic of his own. Since the employee was not engaged in the carrying out of any duties which his employment imposed upon him, under general principles of law the master would not be liable for the acts of his employee under the circumstances. It is true, however, that the master may be held liable for injuries to persons resulting from the incompetence or unfitness of a servant where the master was negligent in selecting or retaining an incompetent or unfit servant. . . . In such a case the master's negligence in hiring or retaining the incompetent or unfit servant makes him liable to the injured party. Furthermore, every assault upon a third person or guest is not necessarily out of the scope of the employee's employment.

It is thus well to note that the employer may be negligent in initially hiring one who is unfit if he can be charged with this knowledge.

A hotel must exercise care in overseeing its employees. What, specifically, is proper supervision will of course vary and depend to large extent upon the situation. The nature of the task the employee is assigned to, and perhaps the employee himself, may bear upon the supervision required. If the business fails to supervise properly and as a result of this failure so to do a guest is injured, the business may be held responsible for the damages sustained. An Illinois case is an example wherein a hotel bellboy had been drinking while on duty. The bellboy somehow obtained a passkey and used it to gain entry to the room of the female plaintiff who was a guest at the hotel. Once inside the room the bellboy raped the female guest, then left. The plaintiff sued the hotel for damages. On appeal a judgment against the hotel for $25,000.00 was upheld. In *Danile v. Oak Park Arms Hotel Inc.* [203 N.E.2d 706 (Ill. App. 1965)] the court stated:

> There was evidence presented at the trial that Mulligan had been drinking while on duty and that he was absent from his post for two periods of about one hour each. There was evidence that in order to get the pass key to the rooms, Mulligan had to pass near a switchboard operator and a night attendant who could have determined that he had been drinking while on duty. We do not say that the evidence on these points is conclusive, but evidence was such that a jury might reasonably come to the conclusion that the hotel staff could have and should have known of Mulligan's absence from his post when he was upstairs drinking and they should have found out where he was. There was some evidence that the staff should have seen Mulligan go in and take the pass key, and a jury could reasonably find negligence in that they should have guarded this key more carefully and did not. Whether we agree with the jury's conclusion or not, we have no basis for substituting our opinion of the evidence for the one it gave.

At this point it is well to summarize what has been previously considered in this chapter. The operator of a hotel or motel, much as any other business, is generally held legally responsible for injuries to third persons or guests that are caused by acts of his employees, which acts are within the course and scope of their employment. The legal doctrine under which the employer is held vicariously liable is respondeat superior. While many rationales for such liability have been proposed, it is today really more of a policy judgment of risk allocation by many courts than anything else.

What acts of employees are "within the scope of employment" is a frequently raised question. Some general guidelines have been furnished. Certainly everyday, routine duties are to be so considered. Other acts may or may not be; the further removed the act is from being related to the job or duties of the employee or a motivation to serve the employer's interests, the less likely the act is held within the scope of employment. Ultimately each individual case will be decided upon its own facts, the determination normally being for the jury.

When the employee deviates substantially from duties related to his employment and causes injury it is less likely that the employer is to be held legally liable. He should not be when the employee has acted strictly for his own benefit with no desire to serve the employer's interest. In such a case respondeat superior would have little application, though other legal concepts conceivably may.

An employer should exercise care in selection and training of his employees as well, for it is through them that he acts in many instances. Under the previously discussed concepts of law the employer may be held responsible for the employees' actions though he was not even present at the time of the action. Moreover, the employer may be found directly negligent in hiring or retaining a person as an employee whom he knows, or with the exercise of reasonable care should know, is potentially dangerous. Thus when the employer has knowledge that an employee has a very bad temperament and has been involved in prior assaults, then the *employer* may be found negligent in continuing to employ such person, at least in a position where others would be exposed to harm.

There are, of course, many other occurrences that may lead to legal liability for a business other than acts of its employees or servants. An individual or business may also be responsible for acts of animals that it owns or controls. In closing this chapter let us consider a Pennsylvania case involving a bar and a dog. That case recognized an innkeeper's responsibility to provide safety from acts of employees of the inn, and others, but it at the same time considered a somewhat different situation, the business owner's liability for the act of his dog. The plaintiff entered a tavern open to the public and operated by the defendant. Plaintiff ordered a beer, then asked to use the men's room. There was conflict in the evidence as to exactly what happened subsequently, but it was clear plaintiff was bitten by a dog owned by the defendant and on defendant's premises. In *Poulos v. Brady* (74 A.2d 694) the court wrote:

> In our opinion the case was clearly for the jury. The controlling principle relied upon by plaintiff is clearly stated in Rommel v. Schambacher 120 Pa. 579, 11 A.779 "Where one enters a saloon or tavern, opened for the entertainment of the public, the proprietor is bound to see that he is properly protected from the assaults or insults, as well of those who are in his employ, as of the drunken and vicious men whom he may choose to harbor." . . . Paraphrasing the aforesaid principle, the learned judge of the court below said: "If there is liability for acts of human beings who act like dogs then there should be no question about the liability for acts of dogs, particularly when they belong to the innkeeper." He added: "It was clearly for the jury to decide whether the defendant had discharged her duty by allowing a large dog to roam on the premises, particularly in view of the puppies about which it might feel apprehensive and protective."

Thus a business must certainly exercise care if it keeps a watch dog on the premises, for should the dog cause injury to another person it may be held responsible for such injuries. There may, of course, be some mitigating factors, and the facts again will be of extreme importance.

CHAPTER 7

ACTS OF THIRD PERSONS

THE hospitality industry, much as business in general, is today generally more aware of and concerned with the need for security with respect to its operations, its property, and its patrons. A rising crime rate involving offenses against person and property is partly responsible for this increased awareness, but also in large part it is due to the increasing number of lawsuits involving hotels and motels and the issue of security for guests and patrons. In the last chapter the liability of an establishment for acts of its employees that caused injury to a guest was considered, along with the legal rationale. This chapter will examine the question of a hotel or motel's liability to its guest because of injury or loss inflicted by some third party. Frequently such a third party is some stranger involved in perpetrating a criminal act, but it might also conceivably be another patron of the establishment. Should the establishment be liable in such a case? The answer to this question depends to a large extent upon the circumstances, surrounding the incident.

The injury of a guest of a hotel by either another guest or some other, often unknown, party does not automatically render the hotel liable to the guest for injury or loss sustained. The legal concept of strict liability is not here applied; some fault on the part of the hotel must be shown. Some act or failure to act of the hotel must have been a cause of the injury or loss. Without such a showing the party seeking to recover will likely fail. It is a generally recognized concept that an innkeeper is *not* an insurer of the safety of its guests. [See *Black v. Heininger* 163 So.2d 3 (Fla. App. 1964); *Nixon v. Royal Coach Inn of Houston* 464 S.W.2d 900 (Tex. Civ. App. 1971).]

Many cases involve the guest suing the hotel or motel after the guest has been the victim of a criminal assault occurring on the property owned or controlled by the hotel. It has been held that the owner or operator of the hotel is not liable for the conduct of another person on his premises who causes injury to a business invitee, such as a guest, unless the owner or operator has notice that a danger is presented and an opportunity to protect against it. The reader is referred to the case of *Highlands Ins. Co. v. Gilday* [398 So.2d 834 (Fla. App. 1981)]. In that case the defendant owned and operated a hotel in which the plaintiff alleged that he was assaulted in the ground floor men's room of the hotel. Based upon the evidence presented the plaintiff was held not entitled to recover against the hotel because he had failed to prove any breach of duty on the part of the defendant. The plaintiff failed to show that there had been any adequate notice to the defendant hotel of the need for security measures in this particular case.

Notice of the need for security measures at a hotel could come in many ways. Certainly the occurrence of prior problems on the premises should be construed as a need for protective measures to be taken. Ignoring prior situations involving attacks against guests is a serious mistake on the part of management; once the existence of problems is put on notice some action should be taken. Specifically what measures are taken and the adequacy of those measures must be determined on a case by case basis.

The requirement of an innkeeper to exercise ordinary and reasonable care to protect his or her guests is a widely recognized proposition. This applies to protection from criminal acts of others, but again, the hotel is *not* made an insurer of safety. It is not held to guarantee that a guest will not be injured by the criminal act of another. In a case arising in Florida, the plaintiffs, husband and wife, were guests at a large hotel owned and operated by the defendant corporation. When the plaintiffs returned to their room after an outing they were attacked by three men who had somehow gained access to their room. The plaintiff wife in resisting was beaten up, and both husband and wife were tied up and gagged. A small amount of jewelry and cash was then taken from them. The plaintiffs subsequently filed a lawsuit against the hotel corporation alleging that the hotel had failed to provide adequate security personnel for the protection of its guests and that it had allowed unknown persons to have access to room keys. In discussing the duty of a hotel to protect its guests the court wrote, in *Phillips Petroleum Co. v. Dorn* [292 So.2d 429 (Fla. App. 1974)],

> A registered guest in a hotel is a business invitee to whom the hotel owes a duty of reasonable care for their safety. . . . While most of the Florida cases announcing the innkeeper-guest standard of care involve a hotel's common rooms and other facilities which are available for the use of all hotel guests in common, we see no reason to require a higher degree of care for protection of a guest in the confines of the particular room assigned to him upon registration, than in the common areas. As pointed out by the Supreme Court in the recent case of Wood v. Camp, Fla. 1973, 284 So.2d 691, persons entering the premises of another fall into one of three categories, trespassers, licensees, or invitees. Each category has a standard of care ascribed to it by law which constitutes a guideline by which to test the negligence vel non of the possessor of the land, and the standard of care owed to an occupant of a hotel room (an invitee) is reasonable care.

The major question posed, then, is what is reasonable and ordinary care to be exercised by the hotel or motel in a given case. What are they to be expected to do? What precautions will constitute sufficient care? It will, of course, vary from situation to situation. Certainly, though, it would appear that providing such things as adequate latches and locks on room doors to secure the room against unauthorized entry would be reasonably expected of an establishment. This is very basic so far as security precautions are concerned. Another Florida case appeared to be largely concerned with this particular question. In *Rosier v. Gainesville Inns Assoc. Ltd.* [347 So.2d 1100 (Fla. App. 1977)] the plaintiffs had rented two rooms at the defendant's hotel, one for their children and one for themselves. Shortly after the plaintiffs retired for the evening they locked their door but did not secure the chain latch on the inside. During the early morning hours they awoke to find an intruder in the room, and a scuffle with this person ensued. One of the plaintiffs was stabbed twice, though fortunately not seriously wounded. At this point the intruder escaped, apparently leaving a key on a leather strap lying on the floor, one much like the motel maids carried. To the shock of the plaintiffs this intruder returned, grabbed the key, and fled once again. At the later trial of the case a security expert testified that the locks on the motel doors were of a low grade, a better type being recommended. A judgement for the defendant motel was reversed on appeal. Relevant parts of the *Rosier* opinion follow:

> The court stated the failure by the Gainesville Holiday Inn to use adequate locks could not reasonably be considered the cause of the Rosiers' injuries. He found that since the Rosiers failed to secure the chain latch to the outside door, one could not reasonably assume the Rosiers would have used the dead bolt latch had the mortise lock been available. Such a conclusion could only be reached by the jury.[1] It is clear that upon a motion for directed verdict, all reasonable inferences are construed in favor of the nonmoving party. . . . There is of course the question of foreseeability. Could the motel reasonably foresee that the failure to use adequate locks would lead to the sort of injury sustained here? Here there was some evidence of illegal entries into unoccupied motel rooms. Indeed, the motel manager was questioned concerning a police incident report stating that persons unknown entered a nearby room of the motel, probably with the aid of a passkey. That report was made some five months before this incident. It is clear that the motel licensee had knowledge of prior burglaries of guests' rooms carried out in a manner similar to that shown by plaintiffs. A registered guest in a hotel or motel is a business invitee to whom the innkeeper owes a duty of reasonable care for his safety. *Americana of Bal Harbour Inc. v. Kiester,* 245 So.2d 121 (Fla.3rd DCA 1971).

Thus it is seen that in this case the court ruled it a question for the jury as to the adequacy of locks on the doors that were provided by the defendant hotel.

Aside from provision of proper physical devices to secure entry to rooms, other acts of an establishment may require careful examination as to their sufficiency. Even the question of the location of a guest's assigned room on the premises has been raised in court. In at least one case it was alleged that the establishment was negligent because of the room assignment it had made to the plaintiff. In the case of *Nixon v. Royal Coach Inn of Houston* [464 S.W.2d 900 (Tex. Civ. App. 1971)] the female plaintiff checked in at the hotel in the evening hours after making a long drive during the day. When she went to her room she was attacked by an unknown assailant. Subsequently she filed suit against the hotel, alleging that the hotel had been negligent in the room assignment that it had made to her. It was plaintiff's theory that it was negligent for the hotel to assign a lone female guest to a room in what was alleged was a remote part of the hotel complex. The court did not, however, hold the hotel liable, it stating that it could find no requirement on the part of an innkeeper to assign a guest to any particular room or part of a hotel establishment.

Attacks upon guests do not just occur in the room assigned to the guests, but they have unfortunately occurred in other parts of hotels as well. If an attack occurs on property owned and controlled by the hotel then it will certainly be a concern of the business. A Texas case involved an incident in the parking lot of a hotel. The plaintiff was attending a business convention at the defendant's hotel. He had paid the fee and parked in a parking lot owned by the defendant, which was located in front of the hotel. After spending an evening at the convention activity in the hotel the plaintiff left at approximately 11:30 PM and walked to the parking lot to his automobile. At that time two unknown assailants beat, stabbed, and robbed the plaintiff. As a result of these acts the plaintiff sued the hotel, alleging that it was negligent in failing to provide adequate security in some form. In its defense the hotel argued that the acts of the unknown criminal assailants were a new and intervening cause of the plaintiff's injury, and that this was not associated with any act or failure to act on the part of the hotel. A judgement of the trial court in favor of the defendant hotel was reversed on appeal, and the case was remanded for a new trial. In doing so in *Walkoviak v. Hilton Hotels Corp.* [580 S.W.2d 623 (Tex. Civ. App. 1979)] the court stated:

> The proprietor of a public business establishment has the duty to exercise reasonable care to protect his patrons from intentional injuries caused by third persons if he has reason to know that such acts are likely to occur, either generally or at some particular time. Liability for injuries may arise from the failure of the proprietor to exercise reasonable care to discover that such acts by third persons are occurring, or are likely to occur, coupled with the failure to provide reasonable means to protect his patrons from the harm or to give a warning adequate to enable the patrons to avoid the harm. . . . The injury to appellant resulted from criminal acts of persons who invaded the premises of the innkeeper. Such invasion by criminals is an occurrence which the security measures of a hotel should reasonably be designed to prevent.

A Wisconsin case examined various factors to be taken into consideration in determining whether a hotelkeeper had exercised ordinary care for the protection and safety of his guests. In that case a former employee of a motel entered its lobby to talk to some of the present employees, then entered its kitchen and stole a bellboy's shirt. Subsequently he and another person sought entry to one of the motel rooms, claiming that its telephone was out of order. When denied entry they attempted the same ploy at the room of the plaintiff. The plaintiff opened the door and was then robbed. Fortunately a local police officer had observed the actions of these criminals, and the police officer and others arrived to arrest them shortly thereafter. In *Peters v. Holiday Inns, Inc.* [278 N.W.2d 208 (Wis. 1979)] the court discussed the care owed by a hotel to its guests. In part, it was stated:

> In our mobile society, travellers carry sums of money because of necessity and the problems caused by the lack of adequate identification for cashing checks in areas away from home. Thus, innkeepers should foresee that necessarily large amounts of monies and credit cards are carried by their guests and consequently increased security is required in these days of rapidly increasing assaultive crimes. Certainly hotel patrons can expect that reasonable security will be provided, combined with the friendliness, hospitality and graciousness so widely advertised by modern hotels.
>
> In *Osborne v. Montgomery,* 203 Wis. 223, 242-43, 234 N.W. 372, (1971), it was noted that once a legal duty has been imposed, the standard of care to be exercised is defined in the following language:
>
> > " . . . the degree of care which the great mass of mankind ordinarily exercises under the same or similar circumstances. A person fails to exercise ordinary care when, without intending to do any wrong, he does an act or omits a precaution under circumstances in which a person of ordinary intelligence and prudence ought reasonably to foresee that such act or omission will subject him or his property, or the person or property of another to an unreasonable risk of injury or damage."
>
> Thus, the conduct of hotel innkeepers in providing security must conform to the standard of ordinary care. In the context of the hotel-guest relationship, it is foreseeable that an innkeeper's failure to maintain adequate security measures not only permits but may even encourage intruders to rob or assault hotel patrons. Therefore, we hold that a hotel has a duty to exercise ordinary care to provide adequate protection for its guests and their property from assaultive and other types of criminal activity. Thus, in meeting its standard of ordinary care a hotel must provide security commensurate with the facts and circumstances that are or should be apparent to the ordinarily prudent person. In other words, an innkeeper's standard of care in providing security will vary according to the particular circumstances and location of the hotel.

Accordingly, as the degree of care that an innkeeper must exercise will vary in relation to the attendant circumstances, relevant factors in deciding whether a hotel has exercised ordinary care in providing adequate security are: industry standards, the community's crime rate, the extent of assaultive or criminal activity in the area or in similar business enterprises; the presence of suspicious persons, and the peculiar security problems posed by the hotel's design. A hotel's liability depends upon the danger to be apprehended and the presence or absence of security measures designed to meet the danger. The particular circumstances may require one or more of the following safety measures: a security force, closed circuit television surveillance, dead bolt and chain locks on the individual rooms as well as security doors on hotel entranceways removed from the lobby area.

Consequently, we apply the ordinary care standard to the facts of this case in determining whether the defendant motel was entitled to summary judgment. The plaintiff's primary contentions are that the motel was negligent in: (1) allowing suspicious persons to roam about the premises unsupervised during the early morning hours; (2) permitting the suspicious person to gain access to the Holiday Inn uniforms thus enabling the man to pose as a hotel employee; (3) as it is not necessary to pass by the motel lobby, the motel failed to provide security personnel, television monitoring equipment or other security devices, including locks on the outside doors leading to the hallways in the separated motel building where Rooms Nos. 143 and 185 were located so as to prevent ingress to all but motel patrons. The trial court described these contentions as "potentially valid" but nonetheless concluded the evidentiary facts did not raise competing inferences which would sustain a verdict in favor of the plaintiff.

We hold, based upon the applicability of the established duty of ordinary care imposed on a hotel to provide security, and the facts and circumstances presented by the parties, reasonable persons could draw competing inferences as to whether the defendant motel provided adequate security. The present case raises a jury question as to whether or not the presence of the assailant in the motel lobby, not for purposes of renting a room, but looking for a certain motel employee at 3:00 a. m. was a suspicious circumstance requiring the motel staff to monitor the intruder's whereabouts.

Further, in this case a jury may draw different conclusions over whether the motel was compelled to have locks, security personnel or television monitoring equipment in the entranceway to the separated structure, even though the affidavits indicate the police have been sparingly called because of past security problems. It is conceivable that a jury may conclude these precautions were necessary since the presence of unauthorized persons in the separated building cannot be discovered from the lobby desk.

To this point the cases discussed have involved assaults upon a hotel guest by a stranger engaged in the commission of a criminal act. As pointed out the courts generally recognize that a duty to exercise ordinary and reasonable care for the safety of the guest is imposed upon the hotel. Specific precautions to be taken will vary depending upon the circumstances. The basic need for adequate locks on rooms has been noted. In some cases reasonable care may require that other measures be taken. It may be desirable to employ security guards, perhaps install some type of closed circuit surveillance of the hotel premises, construct physical barriers such as fences to restrict access to the premises to authorized persons, and made certain that lighting is adequate. A hotel's location, previous experiences involving criminal conduct on its premises, and other factors are important in determining if existing precautions are indeed adequate and if not what should be done.

When a hotel or motel has previously experienced security problems, particularly recurring ones, it is on notice that perhaps its precautions are inadequate and will not sufficiently protect its guests. If it fails then to take reasonable steps to reduce the likelihood of future such occurrences then it is failing to do what is required of it for the legitimate safety of invitees on its grounds. In large measure a commonsense approach to the problem may be helpful. Obviously, smaller establishments will not have the economic resources to use some sophisticated technical systems, but there are many measures that can be taken at relatively low cost. Keeping track of persons on the hotel premises, making inquiry of the business or purpose of those not guests, and providing adequate lighting for parking lots and common areas after dark are some of the fundamental security measures that can be taken to make the environment safer for guests. Aside from aiding the defense of a hotel in case of a lawsuit, having taken reasonable measures for the safety of guests is simply good business and good public relations.

A guest's claim against an inn may arise as a result of an injury sustained due to the act of another guest or patron of the business. Is the innkeeper responsible for such acts? Not in an absolute manner; the law does not make the hotel an insurer of the guest's safety, as previously stated. However, much as it must exercise ordinary care to protect its guests from criminal acts of strangers, it also is under a duty to exercise reasonable care to protect against harm from other patrons. A Kansas case is illustrative. The plaintiffs had been together for a business conference, had dinner, and then stopped at a bar and ordered a pitcher of beer. While there they were subsequently assaulted by another group of unruly patrons who had been at the tavern for some time drinking, brawling, and harassing others. The court in writing an opinion considered what the duty of a business operator was with respect to protecting his customers from attack by other customers. It is of value to examine part of the court's opinion in *Kimple v. Foster* [469 P.2d 281 (Kan. 1970)] in which the court felt sufficient evidence had been presented to establish notice to the operator of the tavern of potential danger to guests:

> The basis of the plaintiffs' claims against Mr. Foster, the proprietor of The Roaring Sixties, was his failure to provide them with the protection to which they were entitled as his guests. There is actually little dispute between plaintiffs and defendant with respect to the general proposition that a tavern operator owes his patrons the duty to exercise reasonable care for their personal safety. In this jurisdiction the general rule has been phrased in Huddleston v. Clark, 186 Kan. 209, 349 P.2d 888, in these words:
>
> > "While the owner and operator of a public tavern and grill is held to a stricter accountability for injuries to patrons than is the owner of private premises generally, the rule is that he is not an insurer of the patrons, but owes them only what, under the particular circumstances, is ordinary and reasonable care."
>
> . . . the defendant asserts that the record is entirely bereft of evidence which would tend to place him on notice of impending danger. In making this assertion, we believe the defendant is mistaken. As we view this record, there is ample evidence to have alerted both the defendant himself and his go-go girl manager to the probability of violence erupting from the rowdy and unruly gang which had infested the tavern since afternoon.
>
> We shall make no attempt to set out the evidence in detail. It is sufficient to say that "the guys" around the beer can pyramid, who ranged in number as high as eight or ten, were high and belligerent at 4:30 that afternoon and "maybe wanted to start a fight"; that about 5:15 or so the male manager (Mr. Foster) was in the tavern and set the boys up for a free beer; about 5:30 or 6:00 a fight broke out in which one of the fellows from the "pyramid" table hit and ran another guy out of the tavern; that the group was loud and boisterous and "would have gotten thrown out [of any other bar], because of the noise they were creating and the belligerence or sarcasm toward other people."

> There is further evidence from a member of the gang that Foster's employees knew of this prior fight because they turned on the lights to stop it; and that there was another incident at the tavern over a hat involving some farm boys and one of the gang took the hat and everyone got to joking about it.
>
> Mr. Foster himself testified that he was in the tavern from 5:00 to 6:00 that afternoon; that the boys were then building the pyramid of beer cans; and that he bought the boys a round of free beer.
>
> We think the foregoing evidence was clearly sufficient, if believed by the jury, to warrant the jury in concluding that the defendant Foster, himself, had knowledge of facts which should reasonably have placed him on notice that trouble might well be expected from the unruly, belligerent group, and that an explosion might erupt which would endanger the safety of his patrons.

The operator of an inn, restaurant, or similar business is generally held liable for an assault upon a guest by another patron if the operator had reason to anticipate the assault and failed to exercise reasonable care to prevent it. A tavernkeeper must exercise the care and vigilance that a prudent man would to protect his guests from injury from disorderly acts of other guests. *Reilly v. 180 Club Inc.* 14 N.J.Super 420, 82 A.2d 210.

The steps that an operator is required to take will vary. Disorderly patrons who may pose a danger to others should often be asked to leave. If necessary the appropriate local law enforcement officials should be summoned to maintain order. Failure to take reasonable steps for protection of one patron from acts and assaults of another patron may lead to sizable judgments against a business operator when a patron is seriously injured. See *Reiboldt v. Bedient* [562 P.2d 991] in which there was an award of $75,000.00 arising from an incident in which a patron attacked another. It is not that the innkeeper or tavern operator is being held vicariously liable for the acts of his customers, as he might possibly be for his employees, rather he is held liable for his own failure to exercise reasonable care for his patrons' safety.

CHAPTER 8

SECURITY PERSONNEL

CHAPTER 7 recognized the concept that the operator of a hotel or motel owes a duty to his guests to exercise ordinary and reasonable care for their safety from assault by strangers or other patrons of the establishment. The law does not make the operator a guarantor of his guests' safety, but it does hold that he should take reasonable precautions that are within his power. As discussed, what might be considered reasonable and necessary will vary from case to case, but some generalized steps have been mentioned. One of those steps frequently taken is to arrange for private security personnel to be on and patrol the premises.

When the establishment elects to use private security personnel there are two basic approaches. The business may directly employ its own security force, or it may contract for the provision of security personnel by a firm that specializes in providing such services, and there are today many of these. From strictly a business standpoint there are advantages and disadvantages with either approach. While directly hiring allows the employer to choose the person, it also necessitates that the employer take on the added work of scheduling, training, and other functions. By contracting with an outside firm the employer in large part avoids this. From the legal standpoint of the hotel or motel's liability for the acts of such persons there may be a very substantial difference between the approaches. As there appears to be an increasing volume of litigation involving security guards, this chapter will briefly examine the employer's responsibility for their actions. First to be considered is the situation in which the business has chosen to hire its own security guards.

An employer is generally held vicariously liable for injuries caused by acts of his employees or servants when such acts are held to be within the course and scope of their employment. This is so under the legal doctrine of respondeat superior discussed in the preceeding chapter. With respect to this, security personnel are considered essentially as any other employees would be, and the employer is vicariously liable for their actions. Due to the nature of the employment and duties of security personnel the employer, should give special consideration to their training and supervision. It is certainly foreseeable that at some point they may be required to exercise force against a patron or third person. Thus the employer should adequately instruct these persons with respect to the performance of their duties and see that in the course of the performance they are properly supervised.

Force is often necessary to keep order and protect patrons from injury. Certainly operators of taverns have realized this for many years. However, it has very often led to charges that a person was unnecessarily injured by a "bouncer" or other one charged with keeping order. Unruly persons should be asked to leave, or if they refuse, the local law enforcement authorities should be called in. There are, of course, those times when the situation demands more immediate action. When force is used security personnel should use only that degree of force which is reasonable and necessary under the circumstances. This requires, certainly, the exercise of common sense. Failing to provide adequate security may lead to an employer's liability if a patron is hurt, but so also will a security guard who uses unnecessary force against a person. The factual setting of each situation will be crucial in determining if the guard's actions were proper. It is of value for the employer to explain carefully to those employees charged with keeping order that their use of excessive and unjustified degrees of force can render both the employee and employer liable to an injured party in a lawsuit for damages. In many instances it becomes a judgment call, and a decision to act and how must be made very quickly by the employee. There is no time to sit and think and reflect. Still, it is important that the employee act in a reasonable manner.

Should an employee have been previously involved in assaults or situations in which it appeared that his temper was lost and he caused unnecessary injury to others, the employer must carefully consider the advisability of retaining the employee. After being put on notice from prior incidents that the employee may have an aggressive temperament and pose a threat or danger to others the employer may *himself* be considered negligent in keeping such a person on in a position where patrons or the public is exposed to harm. If a third party is subsequently unnecessarily injured by the said employee's conduct, then the employer's *own* negligence in retaining the employee may be a basis for the employer being held liable to the injured party, as well as vicarious liability in connection with respondeat superior.

May an employer be found to have been negligent in hiring a person initially? The answer to this question would appear to be in the affirmative under certain circumstances. A general statement on the law is found in the Restatement of the Law, Agency, Second at section 213:

> A person conducting an activity through servants or other agents is subject to liability for harm resulting from his conduct if he is negligent or reckless:
> (b) in the employment of improper persons or instrumentalities in work involving risk of harm to others.

The comments to this section indicate that the employer is not liable simply because the employee is careless, unfit, or vicious, but because the employer failed to exercise reasonable care himself under the circumstances in selecting the employee. In general courts seem to accept this proposition. The opinion in *Coath v. Jones* [419 A.2d 1249 (Pa. Super. 1980)] stated:

> The first issue is whether an employer can be negligent as a result of the hiring of an employee who the employer knew, or should have known, had a propensity for violence. The issue has been met in a number of cases with the result that an employer may be negligent if he knew or should have known that his employee had a propensity for violence and such employment might create a situation where the violence would harm a third person.

Due to the nature of a security guard's duties the employer should be especially careful in screening applicants. Specifically what type of background investigation of a potential employee should be made is difficult to say. It would appear desirable to at least contact prior employers. As the potential for harm associated with the position increases, more care should be exercised in selection of employees. As stated by the court in *Easley v. Apollo Detective Agency* [387 N.E.2d 1241 (Ill. App. 1979)], a case involving the hiring of a person to work as an armed security guard with passkeys in an apartment complex:

> Moreover, it has been held that, in the selection of an agent, an employer will be held to the exercise of care reasonably commensurate with the perils and hazards likely to be encountered in the performance of the agent's duty; that is, such care as a reasonably prudent person would exercise in view of the consequences that might reasonably be expected to result if an incompetent, careless, or reckless agent was employed for the particular duty. . . .

In many instances a hotel or motel will provide security guards by contracting with a firm that specializes in providing such services. The security guards thus provided are normally *not* considered employees of the hotel or motel but remain employees of the security firm with which the contract was made. In such a situation the hotel or motel is often not held liable for the negligent or intentional acts of such guards, if the hotel or motel had no knowledge of the dangerous propensities of the guard. [See *Brien v. 18925 Collins Avenue Corp.* 233 So.2d 847 (Fla. App. 1970).] In that case the appellant's deceased, after being stopped by a security guard at a motel in the early morning hours, was shot by the guard. The guard was employed by a private security company that had contracted with the motel's owner to protect and patrol the premises and grounds. In *Brien, supra,* the court said:

> We therefore hold that in the absence of an allegation that the owner had or ought to have had notice of the dangerous propensities of the guard employed by the security corporation, the owner will not be liable for consequences of the allegedly negligent manner in which the employee of the independent contractor performed his duties. We conclude that an owner of real property is not vicariously liable for harm allegedly caused by the negligent discharge of a firearm by an employee of the independent contractor security corporation the owner hires to protect his property.

While the employer hotel/motel is normally not liable for acts of employees of independent contractors there are possible exceptions. Inherent in the idea of an independent contractor is the thought that *it* controls its employees, and not the business with whom it contracts. Thus if the hotel exercises direct control and supervision over guards provided by an independent contractor guard service the hotel may be held liable for acts of the guards. The case of *Fruehauf Corporation v. Aetna Insurance Co.* [336 So.2d 457 (Fla. App. 1976)], while not involving a hotel or motel, illustrates the concept. The court said:

> An employer may also be held liable for the negligence of a guard service where the relationship between the employer and the guard service is one of master-servant rather than employer-independent contractor. The relationship is determined by the right of control concept. When the employer retains the right of control over the personnel supplied, the master-servant relationship is created, and the employer will be held vicariously liable for the negligence of the hired personnel acting within the scope of employment.

Another Florida case illustrates the above. A bar employed an independent contractor to provide security service to it. An employee-guard of the independent contractor was working at the bar one evening and had an altercation with a patron when the guard tried to prevent the unruly patron from removing a glass from the establishment. Outside in the parking lot the patron was shot by the guard. The employer-bar was held liable for the acts of the employee-guard of the independent contractor because the employer-bar was found to have exercised direct control over the guard and the way in which the guard performed his duties. [See *Jax Liquors Inv. v. Hall* 344 So.2d 247 (Fla. App. 1976).] The courts thus appear to be holding that one who controls, directs, or supervises the duties or performance of a guard who is technically employed by an independent contractor/security service may be held liable for the acts of the guard when a third party is injured. In essence the de facto relationship between the two has become one of master-servant, similar to if the guard were directly employed.

CHAPTER 9

INJURIES INVOLVING PHYSICAL FACILITIES

INJURIES occurring on the premises of a hotel or motel have given rise to a great deal of litigation. Such injuries have involved a wide range of situations, from a slip and fall to a guest or invitee sustaining harm from using an allegedly defective piece of furniture or equipment. Frequently the guest or invitee who has been injured seeks to recover by alleging that his injury was the result of the establishment creating and/or allowing a dangerous condition to exist on its premises. It should be noted, of course, that the condition need not have been caused by the hotel or motel for it to be held liable. It may be found negligent if it knew or reasonably should have known of the condition and failed to take steps to correct it or precautions to warn of it. In general a business establishment that is open to the public owes a duty to maintain its premises in a condition that is safe for those persons invited onto them. What should be done with regard to maintaining premises will vary depending upon the situation. To an extent the type of premises and facilities involved and the persons using them will be important in this determination.

While situations will vary quite substantially, some general observations may be made. Walkways, lobbies, patios, and other common areas where guest traffic is to be expected should be kept in good and clean condition. Water debris, slippery agents, and other foreign substances that might cause a person to fall should not be allowed to remain. Moreover, employees should be trained to look actively for such hazards and see that they are removed. It would also be a desirable practice for a routine periodic inspection of the premises to be made to discover if hazards exist. The longer a hazard is proven to have been allowed to exist on the premises the greater is the potential for the business to be found negligent.

Furnishings, fixtures, and the hotel property in general should be kept in repair and serviceable condition. If an article is found to be defective it should be replaced or put out of service. The hotel property should not only be kept up, the grounds and such should be examined to see if lighting is adequate. Dimly lighted areas, especially where there are steps or ledges, often lead to slip and fall problems. Ledges and drop-offs should often have a railing provided. Mechanical devices should be examined to ascertain that they are functioning properly; a malfunctioning elevator or escalator may cause serious injury.

A general statement of the duty that is imposed upon a hotel or motel for maintaining premises is set forth by the court in *Golden v. Lipkind* [49 So.2d 539 (Fla. 1950)]. In that case the plaintiff was a guest at the hotel operated by the defendant. While on her way to her room she was walking down a dark, unlighted hallway in the hotel and tripped over a mattress that had been left in the hallway. A judgment was entered in favor of the defendant hotel, but on appeal it was reversed. In so doing the court said:

> The law imposes on hotels, apartments, innkeepers, etc. the duty to keep their buildings, premises and appliances in a condition reasonably safe for the use of their guests, or at least those parts of the buildings and premises to which the guests are invited or may reasonably be expected to use. The duty of maintaining safe premises and appliances cannot be delegated to another. There is a duty to exercise ordinary or reasonable care to keep the hallways and passageways reasonably well lighted and free of obstructions or hazards. An innkeeper is not an insurer of the personal safety of his guests arising out of the condition of the buildings and premises.

Slip and fall cases are relatively common types of cases, not only with respect to hotels and motels but other businesses as well. The question of adequate lighting on the premises where the fall occurred is frequently raised as an important issue. By failing adequately to light halls and other areas where guests may be expected a hotel is inviting problems; inadequate lighting has been considered negligence in many instances. In a case similar to the one discussed above the plaintiff/guest tripped over some linoleum and carpeting that hotel employees had removed from a room and left in the hallway. It was held that the hotel had a duty to its guests to exercise ordinary care to keep passageways well lighted and free from objects over which guests might trip and fall. [*Burgauer v. McClellan* 265 S.W. 439.]

The responsibility of properly maintaining the premises is generally recognized, and where the hotel is found negligent in not doing so it is liable to a guest who is injured as a result of its failure. However, this duty may not necessarily extend to the entire physical complex controlled by the establishment. Speaking of the duty to maintain facilities in *Hillman Hotel Inc. v. McHaley* [38 So.2d 566 (Ala. 1949)] the court stated:

> This duty extends to all portions of the premises to which a guest has a right to go and to which it may be reasonably expected that he will go. . . . However, when the injury occurs at a place in the hotel where the guest or patron had no right to be or it was not to be reasonably expected that he would go, then the hotel owes him no duty except that of refraining from active negligence rendering the premises dangerous.

Thus the court was not imposing as great a degree of care upon the business with respect to those areas which would be off limits to guests and where they would have no reason to go, a rational and commonsense consideration.

As mentioned, an innkeeper is not an insurer of the safety of his guests. Simply because an accident occurs *on* his property does not necessarily mean that he is to be automatically held liable for injuries. Normally, to be held liable some negligence on his part must be established. Without a showing of some fault he is not responsible. This is not to imply that he must be responsible for existence of the problem; he may simply have failed to do anything about it once knowledge of it can be charged to him. Actual knowledge of a dangerous condition is not always necessary either. If it has existed for a sufficiently long period the innkeeper may still be held liable for allowing it to continue or failing to warn of it: hence the prior suggestion that the hotel or motel premises be periodically inspected. With regard to slip and fall cases, in one instance on a showing that the innkeeper had *constructive* knowledge that the sidewalks between his motel and restaurant were very slippery and he failed to remove a patch of ice that was concealed from view, he was held liable for injury sustained when a guest fell. (See *Corley v. Andrews* 349 S.W.2d 395.) Certainly if a situation exists on the premises that has previously caused problems then the hotel is on notice of it and should attempt to rectify it. Failure to take appropriate corrective steps will most likely be held to be negligence on the part of the business.

In many other cases where knowledge of a hazard was *not* shown to be imputed to a hotel, the hotel was not found to be negligent. An innkeeper was held *not* liable to an invitee for injuries sustained when the invitee slipped in water on a lavatory floor. In that case it was not shown that the innkeeper had actual knowledge of the dangerous condition, or that it had existed for a long enough time that he would be charged with knowledge of it. (*Crawford v. Pacific States Sav. & Loan Co.* 71 P.2d 333.) Very often the length of time for which a hazard is proven to have existed is of critical importance.

In a case arising in Florida the plaintiff/guest stepped out of an automobile owned by the defendant hotel onto the hotel driveway and slipped and fell, allegedly on some oil or grease on the driveway. In a suit for damages a judgment in favor of the defendant hotel was affirmed on appeal. In *Goldman v. Hollywood Beach Hotel Company* [244 F.2d 413 (C.A. 5 1957)] the court said:

> If it be assumed that the evidence of the appellant has established, prima facie, that he slipped on oil or grease in the driveway at the appellee's hotel and was injured as the result of a fall, we must find, if recovery is to be permitted, evidence of the appellee's negligence. There is no evidence that the oil or grease was placed upon the driveway by any of appellee's employees or that any of them knew of its presence, nor was it shown that the oil or grease had been on the driveway long enough to charge the appellee with knowledge of its presence. Absent such evidence the negligence of the appellee has not been shown.

A Louisiana case involving a guest falling on an outside walkway again illustrates that the mere occurrence of an accident on the property does not render the hotel liable. The case of *Newell v. Zurich Insurance Company* [325 So.2d 745 (La. App. 1976)] involved a minor plaintiff who slipped and fell on an outside walkway at a motel, which walkway was wet from rain. The court held that there was no presumption of negligence on the part of the motel merely by there being presented proof of the fall occurring:

> A user of outside walkways is presumed to see what he should have seen and certainly the presence of water on the streets and sidewalks is obvi-

> ous. . . . Those present agree that the water on the sidewalk where young Newell fell caused the area to be slippery. To conclude, however, that a landlord is under a duty to keep all of his outside walkways free from rainwater would impose an impossible burden. We hold, therefore, that where it is proven that an invitee falls in rainwater on an outside walkway that a presumption of negligence on the part of the landowner does not exist. Further, we find no proof in this regard of negligence on the part of the innkeeper. There is no evidence that the demonstration area which had been covered with an abrasive material had any causal relation with this accident.

The court felt the accident in this case was only a result of the plaintiff's voluntary actions and not of any negligence of the motel.

There are many other types of accidents other than slips and falls that could occur and have occurred in hotels. Some relatively serious accidents have involved persons who have walked into or through glass sliding doors. Sometimes as a defense the hotel has claimed that the guest was contributorily negligent. Whether or not this is the case depends on the facts of the situation. In *Harold Corporation v. Herzberg* [110 So.2d 683 (Fla. App. 1959)] such a question arose. The plaintiff guest had gone to the hotel coffee bar for refreshments. The coffee bar was adjacent to the beach and a recreation area. A part of the walls of the bar was sliding glass panels. There were no handles or markings on the center panel. Testimony in the case indicated that these sliding doors were freely moved to provide wind shields or allow ventilation as need arose. Under these circumstances of the glass panels being unmarked the injured guest was held not contributorily negligent.

Businesses using sliding glass doors should take precautions to see that they are adequately marked with eye-catching decals or that their presence is clearly indicated in some other manner. The risk of serious injury from walking into, or through, such a glass door is great. In *Waugh v. Duke Corporation* [248 F.Supp. 626 (M.D.N.C. 1966)], a case involving a child walking into a motel's glass door, it was stated:

> This Court has also found as a fact that the defendant motel was not negligent in utilizing the type of glass, i.e. crystal plate of the thickness which it employed in the panels. The negligence of the defendant therefore consists of something other than its employment of defective or unsafe material in the construction of its motel and that negligence, the Court finds, consists of the failure of the defendant to warn (plaintiff) of

> the potential danger of the glass panels adjacent to the east door of the room or to place on said panels some marking, device or some guard in front thereof which would prevent a child from inadvertently walking thereinto.

In those establishments using such glass panels on parts of their business premises it becomes incumbant to take reasonable steps to give guests notice of the panel. One that has no decals, markings, or handles on it readily to mark it as a solid glass door or window may be held to present an unreasonable risk to guests. To mark such panels adequately takes minimal effort by hotel management, but it may be of great value in a later suit.

Many other types of hotel fixtures have been involved in accidents in which a guest has been injured. As a general proposition the hotel is held responsible for keeping such fixtures in working order and in a state of repair. The case of *Hillinghorst v. Heart of Atlanta Motel Inc.* [122 S.E.2d 751 (Ga. App. 1961)] was a case involving a guest at the motel being injured in a bathtub. The plaintiff/guest was in the tub taking a bath and was injured when attempting to get out of the tub. Mounted on the wall next to the tub was a porcelain soap dish and above that was a porcelain handle about 6 inches long, mounted on the wall. The purpose of the handle was so that one in the tub could hold onto it and use it to assist in getting up. The plaintiff took hold of the handle and started to pull himself up from the tub, but the handle crumbled and caused plaintiff to be injured. The question of whether or not the motel was negligent in having failed to discover the condition of the handle was properly for a jury to decide. The court stated:

> The question of a violation of "the duty to exercise ordinary care to afford (guests) premises that are reasonably safe for use and occupancy," which is the duty an innkeeper owes his guests, is a question of negligence and this court is bound by the rule that such matters are for the jury except in plain, palpable and indisputable cases. . . . Further, the innkeeper has a duty to inspect and is liable for such injuries caused by defects as would be disclosed by a reasonable inspection. . . . Thus plaintiff's case is for the jury and it was error to sustain the oral motion to dismiss. . . .

A hotel or motel is in control of its premises, rooms, and furnishings. It daily seeks to clean and maintain the premises. Through its employees, it has the opportunity to inspect its facilities and furnishings to ascertain that they are in fact safe. With this opportunity to so inspect, if it fails to do so, or if it makes only a cursory and inadequate inspection then it will frequently be held negligent if a guest is hurt because of a fixture or furnishing that is defective and that a reasonable inspection would have shown to be defective. It owes to its guests a duty to make such an inspection. This is not to imply that every piece of furniture must be turned upside down every day; only reasonable care is required. Whether or not the procedures and inspections are in fact reasonable and adequate is for a jury to determine based upon the factual setting of the case. So it was held in *Palagano v. Georgian Terrace Hotel Company* [181 S.E.2d 512 (Ga. App. 1971)], a case involving a guest being injured while using furnishings in his room. Specifically the plaintiff in that case alleged that he was injured when the bed in his room collapsed with him. Evidence was presented that rooms were cleaned and inspected daily, but it was held to be up to the jury to decide if the inspection was adequate to fulfill the defendant motel's duty owed to its guests to provide reasonably safe facilities.

The author does not intend to leave the reader with the impression that an unbearable burden rests upon innkeepers. It has adequately been pointed out that the courts do not make innkeepers insurers of their guests' safety. It is also illustrated well by the preceeding, however, that the innkeeper has the duty to use prudence and ordinary care to provide his guests with safe facilities. If the hotel operator is reasonable in his actions and procedures then his potential for being liable will be significantly reduced. It is of course not possible here to set down absolute guidelines with respect to such concerns as inspection of premises. As indicated, whether or not it is adequate is usually a decision for a jury based upon the particular facts. By here presenting a concept of the innkeeper's general duty and some illustrations it is hoped that the modern hotel or motel operator will become aware of potential problems and take measures in advance to avoid them, or at least reduce the severity of them.

A final case involving injury associated with furniture may be of value. In this Georgia case the plaintiff was a guest at the defendant motel. He sat down in a wood frame lounge chair that was located in his room and that from outward appearances seemed to be in good condition. Unfortunately, when the plaintiff sat down the chair cushion went through the chair and he fell to the floor, injuring his back. It turned out that the cushion fell through because the supporting webbing underneath was missing. The motel denied any actual knowledge of the webbing being absent. Evidence presented indicated that defendant's employees cleaned and inspected the room daily, but that the motel had not received any prior complaints about the chair. A judgment in favor of the guest was upheld on appeal. In its opinion the court in *Gary Hotel Courts Inc. v. Perry* [251 S.E.2d 37 (Ga. App. 1978)] stated:

> The trial court further states: "In the case sub judice, it is undisputed that webbing was missing from the chair bottom, causing the plaintiff to fall and sustain the injury . . . (and) . . . (t)he absence of the webbing could have been discovered by looking under the chair. It was rightfully the province of the jury to determine whether the defendant breached its duty of ordinary care to the plaintiff; that is whether the defect complained of could or should have been discovered by a reasonable inspection." . . . Here there was evidence that defendant's employees cleaned and inspected the rooms daily. This evidence would have authorized the jury to have determined that the defendant was chargeable with notice of any defects which should have been discovered by the exercise of ordinary care and diligence.

Aside from daily cleaning of rooms it would be prudent for the management periodically to take a closer look at such things as furnishings. It would take a relatively limited amount of time actually to inspect and examine furnishings periodically to ascertain their condition and serviceability. When the cost of this action is measured against the potential benefit of perhaps avoiding an injury to a guest, the investment in time is well worth it. Certainly even in the unfortunate event of an injury occurring, periodic inspections should work to the advantage of the hotel in convincing a jury that it has in fact exercised proper care for guests' safety.

Recreational facilities such as swimming pools have been the focal points of many accidents. Having such a facility on the premises for use and enjoyment of guests is very often of substantial benefit to the hotel or motel in attracting guests initially. It will act as a "draw" to many potential lodgers looking for relaxation after a long day on the road. Precautions must be taken, however, to insure that the facility itself is initially safe as constructed, that it is properly maintained and operated, and in many instances that it is adequately supervised.

With respect to the facility itself it should be determined whether it is indeed reasonably safe for use by guests. If there is a potential hazard, at the very minimum a warning should be adequately posted. As an example, if a swimming pool is relatively shallow, warnings to users against diving into the water should be conspicuously posted. These warnings should be posted where they are obvious to all users of the facility. Many very serious injuries have been sustained by persons diving into shallow water. The area and deck surrounding a pool should preferably be one that has a rough surface, thereby not contributing to slips and falls when wet. A slippery, smooth surface would increase the probability of a fall occurring and is to be avoided. It is also generally a wise idea not to have open access to a pool but to have the area fenced with a gate. This will reduce the possibility of an unattended young child reaching the pool and accidentally falling in. Any accessories such as slides into the pool should be carefully positioned and water depth at their location should be sufficient for the safety of a user.

If a pool does not have a lifeguard, then notices to this effect should be prominent. Regardless, it is desirable that some floatation devices, rings, etc. be available in the pool area for emergency use if necessary, even if a guest knows that use of the pool is at his own risk. Rules should generally prohibit food and drink from being brought into the pool area, certainly if the container is breakable. Use of the facility should be supervised, to some extent. If hotel management allows activities to occur and continue that create hazards to other pool users the hotel runs the risk of having liability for potential injuries imposed upon it. The most frequently occurring situation is one in which horseplay posing a danger to others is allowed to continue. For a case involving a similar situation the reader is referred to *Gordon v. Hotel Seville Inc.* (105 So.2d 175).

Other types of physical facilities and furnishings besides those mentioned in this chapter might be discussed. What has been presented is illustrative though of potential problems faced by those in the lodging industry. Being aware of these problems and considering exercising reasonable care to prevent or cure them will go a long way toward reducing the probability of suit such as those discussed herein.

CHAPTER 10

MISCELLANEOUS TOPICS

RATES AND RESERVATIONS

IN the lodging business, as in others, it is desirable that prices of services be clearly stated so that disputes over charges with customers may be avoided. When there is a clear understanding between guest and host as to charges for rooms and other services, then the problem of such disputes is largely avoided. Aside from simply being good business policy to post room rates, state statutes commonly *require* that hotels and motels provide such notices regarding their charges for accommodations. Usually this notice must be posted in each individual unit. It must normally indicate what the rate or charge for the room is, with respect also to the number of persons staying there. If there is a different rate in effect for various times of the year, this also must usually be shown. An example of a typical statute is Florida Statute §509.201(1), reprinted in Appendix D of this book.

As a normal part of their business operations, many hotels and motels regularly accept reservations for accommodations. To the traveling public there is quite frequently a distinct advantage in planning in advance for lodgings. It is common knowledge that in many parts of the country during certain seasons hotel and motel accommodations tend to fill up quickly, often being booked far in advance. This is usually the time of year referred to by the local population as the "tourist season" when lodging accommodations are at a premium, and usually the rentals charged are correspondingly at a premium. To attempt to insure having an acceptable place in which to stay and not unnecessarily disrupting a vacation or business trip, travelers often make advance reservations. From a hotel's standpoint making advance reservations is a way in which to plan for effectively filling its rooms, although there is the risk that those persons making bookings will cancel or simply not show. In light of this, to confirm advance reservations and hold rooms, many establishments will request a deposit in advance on the rooms. Problems can still develop. Sometimes current guests will wish to extend their stay. In attempting to accommodate such persons and at the same time honor advance reservations, the hotel must do some juggling.

Is a hotel liable to a person from whom an advance registration for a room has been taken when the hotel than subsequently refuses to honor the reservation? In a case arising in Hawaii the plaintiffs sought *punitive* damages from a hotel for failure to honor previously made reservations. The appellate court, however, did not feel that an award of such damages was called for. The plaintiffs had made reservations at the defendant hotel for certain dates. Upon their arrival they were refused rooms because the hotel was at the time full. They were transferred to a hotel of somewhat lesser quality. Later the plaintiffs again demanded that the defendant honor their prior reservations but were again refused. The defendant hotel argued that the reservation was not "confirmed" as the defendant had not received a cash deposit from the plaintiffs; the plaintiffs' argument was that the agency making reservations for them had guaranteed the defendant hotel at the minimum, the first night's payment, and thus it was indeed a confirmed reservation. The plaintiffs recovered damages, but the trial court refused to instruct the jury on punitive damages. In its opinion the court wrote in *Dold v. Outrigger Hotel* [501 P.2d 368 (Hawaii 1972)]:

> We now consider count III of plaintiffs' complaint. It has long been recognized that an innkeeper, holding himself out to the public to provide hotel accommodations, is obligated, in the absence of reasonable grounds for refusal, to provide accommodations to all persons upon proper request. . . . This duty traditionally extended to the traveler who presented himself at the inn. However, where the innkeeper's accommodations had been exhausted, the innkeeper could justly refuse to receive an applicant. . . . It is well recognized that punitive damages are recoverable for breach of an innkeeper's duty to his guest where the innkeeper's conduct is deliberate or wanton. . . . We are not aware of any jurisdiction that renders an innkeeper liable on his common law

> duty to accommodate under the circumstances of this case. Consequently, plaintiffs are not entitled to an instruction on punitive damages on count III of their complaint.

Since at the time the hotel did not have any rooms available, the court found no breach of an innkeeper's common law duty to accept all proper persons as guests. While the plaintiffs recovered damages, they were *not* allowed a recovery of punitive damages under these facts.

The previous case involved a dispute with respect to reservations not being honored. In other types of cases and other situations a hotel has been held to pay punitive damages to a plaintiff guest. Such was the situation in *Milner Hotels v. Brent* [207 Miss. 892, 43 So.2d 654 (1949)], involving the ejection of a guest. In that case the manager of the hotel stated to the guest, in the presence of other persons and in a loud voice, "We do not want you here," locked her room, and refused to permit her to remove clothing from it. There was evidence that the action was taken against the guest only because of her association with a certain lawsuit. In a case where the acts on the part of the management were so intentionally performed, it was held that punitive damages were properly allowed.

FOUND PROPERTY

Sometimes questions arise with respect to property "found" on the hotel premises and whether or not the finder or the hotel is entitled to possession of it. Often initially it must be determined whether the item is lost or misplaced property versus abandoned property. A distinction may be drawn even between lost and misplaced property. If property is found under such circumstances and conditions as would indicate that it was *not* placed there voluntarily by the owner, it may be said to be "lost." Finding an article of jewelry on a public sidewalk is an example. Misplaced property is that which is found but circumstances are such as indicate the owner voluntarily placed the property there but forgot it. A briefcase left in a restaurant seat is an example. Many courts would allow a finder of "lost" property to retain possession, though sometimes statutes provide certain conditions be met. The finder of "misplaced" property must usually allow the owner or operator of the premises where found to hold it for the true owner. This is logical in that the owner of misplaced property will in all likelihood return seeking it. In contrast to this, abandoned property is property that the owner has voluntarily parted possession with, also intending to relinquish title to it.

In the case of truly abandoned property, generally the first person to take possession of the property then became the new owner. A finder of lost or misplaced property is often held to be a bailee of the property, holding it for the true owner. Many times the facts and surrounding circumstances are extremely important in determining whether particular property was lost or abandoned. The type of property, its value, where it was found, and whether it appeared to have been concealed all may be of importance. With the above in mind let us now consider who is entitled to the possession of "found" property when there is a contest between hotel and guest or employee. While the facts of each case will be different, the following is a useful discussion.

A case from Virginia presents an interesting situation in which a guest claimed certain property that turned up in his hotel room. The plaintiff returned to his room to prepare for a later dinner and noticed a piece of tissue paper on the dresser. When he looked inside the paper, he found a brooch. As it turned out, the maid cleaning the plaintiff's room had found the jewelry while changing the bed and assumed that it was plaintiff's property. The brooch turned out to be worth between $3,500 and $4,000. Plaintiff left it with the hotel, but the owner never claimed it and plaintiff sued the hotel to have possession turned over to him. A judgment was entered for the hotel. In *Flax v. Monticello Realty Co.* [39 S.E.2d 308 (Va. 1946)] the court said:

> The rights of alleged finders of personal property have not infrequently been the subject of adjudications directly and particularly in other jurisdictions. Almost every cited case has some peculiar feature which distinguishes it, in a more or less important degree, from another. The plaintiff in this case was not the finder of the jewel. He appropriated it and claimed it as his own. We may say at this time that the maid made no claim for it and does not do so. The claimant by mere coincidence found himself in an advantageous position to assert some sort of right thereto. . . . The plaintiff, Flax, has no legal standing as a claimant to the brooch.

The court held that this article of property was mislaid or forgotten and the hotel was in the position of a bailee of it with respect to the true owner.

The case of *Jackson v. Steinberg* [200 P.2d 376 (Ore. 1948); 562] is somewhat similar, but the property involved was "found" by a maid. The maid found eight $100 bills under the paper lining of a dresser drawer after a guest had checked out. She turned the money over to the hotel management. When the owner of the money failed to claim it, the maid made a claim for it as a finder. In a subsequent suit the hotel was held entitled to possession of the money, as a bailee for the true owner.

In some jurisdictions there may be statutes with respect to property left in lodging establishments. An example is Florida Statute §509.191.

> Any property left in a public lodging establishment, other than property belonging to a guest who has vacated the premises without notice to the operator and with an outstanding account, which property remains unclaimed after being held by the establishment for 90 days after written notice to the guest, shall become the property of the establishment.

In those states where the legislature has enacted law for disposition of property, it is, of course, subject to interpretation by the courts.

LOSS OF FORMER GUEST'S PROPERTY

Earlier in this book the responsibility, both common law and statutory, for loss of a guest's property while staying at a hotel or motel has been examined. What liability may a hotelkeeper have for property left behind by a guest? As above indicated, this could be considered misplaced property and, if the hotel takes possession of it, then it could be viewed as a bailee of the property, holding it for the true owner. A Florida case considered whether the statute in that state limited a hotel's liability for loss of a former guest's property as well as current guests'. In *Great American Insurance Company v. Coppedge* [405 So.2d 732 (Fla. App. 1981)] the hotel took into custody jewelry left behind by a guest in her room after she had checked out. Subsequently the jewelry was lost. It was held that the hotel's liability for loss of the jewelry *was* limited to $500 under the applicable statute, even though the hotel had not given the guest a receipt as required.

(Practically, under the facts it could not have given a receipt anyway.) The guest had also failed to deposit the items with the hotel or supply an inventory of items to it as required.

Many other topics might have been explored in this chapter. From those that have been the author hopes to have provoked in the reader a thoughtful outlook with respect to his or her position as an innkeeper.

APPENDIX A

42 U.S.C.A. § 2000 (a,b,c)

(a) All persons shall be entitled to the full and equal enjoyment of the goods, services, facilities, privileges, advantages, and accommodations of any place of public accommodation, as defined in this section, without discrimination or segregation on the ground of race, color, religion, or national origin.

(b) Each of the following establishments which serves the public is a place of public accommodation within the meaning of this subchapter if its operations affect commerce, or if discrimination or segregation by it is supported by State action:

(1) any inn, hotel, motel, or other establishment which provides lodging to transient guests, other than an establishment located within a building which contains not more than five rooms for rent or hire and which is actually occupied by the proprietor of such establishment as his residence;

(2) any restaurant, cafeteria, lunchroom, lunch counter, soda fountain, or other facility principally engaged in selling food for consumption on the premises, including, but not limited to, any such facility located on the premises of any retail establishment; or any gasoline station;

(3) any motion picture house, theater, concert hall, sports arena, stadium or other place of exhibition or entertainment; and

(4) any establishment (A)(i) which is physically located within the premises of any establishment otherwise covered by this subsection, or (ii) within the premises of which is physically located any such covered establishment, and (B) which holds itself out as serving patrons of such covered establishment.

(c) The operations of an establishment affect commerce within the meaning of this subchapter if (1) it is one of the establishments described in paragraph (1) of subsection (b) of this section; (2) in the case of an establishment described in paragraph (2) of subsection (b) of this section, it serves or offers to serve interstate travelers or a substantial portion of the food which it serves, or gasoline or other products which it sells, has moved in commerce; (3) in the case of an establishment described in paragraph (3) of subsection (b) of this section, it customarily presents films, performances, athletic teams, exhibitions, or other sources of entertainment which move in commerce; and (4) in the case of an establishment described in paragraph (4) of subsection (b) of this section, it is physically located within the premises of, or there is physically located within its premises, an establishment the operations of which affect commerce within the meaning of this subsection. For purposes of this section, "commerce" means travel, trade, traffic, commerce, transportation, or communication among the several States, or between the District of Columbia and any State, or between any foreign country or any territory or possession and any State or the District of Columbia, or between points in the same State but through any other State or the District of Columbia or a foreign country.

APPENDIX B

Oklahoma Statute Section 503A

15 Okl.St.Ann. § *503a*

"Whenever the proprietor, manager or operator of any hotel, apartment hotel or inn shall provide a safe, vault or other depository for the safekeeping of any money, jewels, ornaments, bank notes, bonds, negotiable securities, or other valuable papers, precious stones, railroad tickets, articles of gold or silver manufacture, or other valuable property of small compass, belonging to guests of said hotel, apartment hotel or inn, and shall notify the guests thereof by posting a notice in a public and conspicuous place and manner in the office or public rooms, or in the public parlors, or in the guest rooms for said hotel, apartment hotel or inn, stating the fact that such safe, vault or other depository is provided, in which such property may be deposited, and if such guest shall neglect to deliver such property to the person in charge of such office, for deposit, in such safe, vault or other depository, the proprietor, manager or operator of such hotel, apartment hotel or inn shall not be liable for any loss of any such property, sustained by such guest, whether by negligence on such proprietor, manager or operator, or his, her, or its servants, or employees, or by fire, theft, burglary or any other cause. Such guest shall, at the time of delivering such property to the person in charge of the office of such hotel, apartment hotel or inn, advise such person of the actual value of such property, and no proprietor, manager or operator or person in charge of the office of such hotel, apartment hotel or inn shall be required to receive property on deposit for safekeeping exceeding Three Hundred Dollars ($300.00) in value; and in case of loss of any such property so deposited for safekeeping, the proprietor, manager or operator of such hotel, apartment hotel or inn shall be liable only for the actual market or pecuniary value of such property, in no event exceeding the sum of Three Hundred Dollars ($300.00). Provided, that the proprietor, manager or operator of any hotel, apartment hotel or inn may, by special agreement in writing with any such guest or guests, receive property of greater value than Three Hundred Dollars ($300.00) and assume liability as shall be provided for in such written agreement."

New York General Business Law sections 200 and 201

§ *200. Safes; limited liability*

Whenever the proprietor or manager of any hotel, motel, inn or steamboat shall provide a safe in the office of such hotel, motel or steamboat, or other convenient place for the safe keeping of any money, jewels, ornaments, bank notes, bonds, negotiable securities or precious stones, belonging to the guests of or travelers in such hotel, motel, inn or steamboat, and shall notify the guests or travelers thereof by posting a notice stating the fact that such safe is provided, in which such property may be deposited, in a public and conspicuous place and manner in the office and public rooms, and in the public parlors of such hotel, motel, or inn, or saloon of such steamboat; and if such guest or traveler shall neglect to deliver such property, to the person in charge of such office for deposit in such safe, the proprietor or manager of such hotel, motel, or steamboat shall not be liable for any loss of such property, sustained by such guest or traveler by theft or otherwise; but no hotel, motel or steamboat proprietor, manager or lessee shall be obliged to receive property on deposit for safe keeping, exceeding five hundred dollars in value; and if such guest or traveler shall deliver such property, to the person in charge of such office for deposit in such safe, said proprietor, manager or lessee shall not be liable for any loss thereof, sustained by such guest or traveler by theft or otherwise, in any sum exceeding the sum of five hundred dollars unless by special agreement in writing with such proprietor, manager or lessee.

§ *201. Liability for loss of clothing and other personal property limited*

1. No hotel or motel keeper except as provided in the foregoing section shall be liable for damage to or loss of wearing apparel or other personal property in the lobby, hallways or in the room or rooms assigned to a guest for any sum exceeding the sum of five hundred dollars, unless it shall appear that such loss occurred through the fault or negligence of such keeper, nor shall he be liable in any sum exceeding the sum of one hundred dollars for the loss of or damage to any such property when delivered to such keeper for storage or safe keeping in the store room, baggage room or other place elsewhere than in the room or rooms assigned to such guest, unless at the time of delivering the same for storage or safe keeping such value in excess of one hundred dollars shall be stated and a written receipt, stating such value shall be issued by such keeper, but in no event shall such keeper be liable beyond five hundred dollars, unless it shall appear that such loss occurred through his fault or negligence, and such keeper may make a reasonable charge for storing or keeping such property, nor shall he be liable for the loss of or damage to any merchandise samples or merchandise for sale, unless the guest shall have given such keeper prior written notice of having the same in his possession, together with the value thereof, the receipt of which notice the hotel or motel keeper shall acknowledge in writing over the signature of himself or his agent, but in any event shall such keeper be liable beyond five hundred dollars, unless it shall appear that such loss or damage occurred through his fault or negligence; . . .

APPENDIX C

Restatement of the Law, Agency 2d Section 229

§ *229. Kind of Conduct within Scope of Employment*

(1) To be within the scope of the employment, conduct must be of the same general nature as that authorized, or incidental to the conduct authorized.

(2) In determining whether or not the conduct, although not authorized, is nevertheless so similar to or incidental to the conduct authorized as to be within the scope of employment, the following matters of fact are to be considered:

- (a) whether or not the act is one commonly done by such servants;
- (b) the time, place and purpose of the act;
- (c) the previous relations between the master and the servant;
- (d) the extent to which the business of the master is apportioned between different servants;
- (e) whether the act is outside the enterprise of the master or, if within the enterprise, has not been entrusted to any servant;
- (f) whether or not the master has reason to expect that such an act will be done;
- (g) the similarity in quality of the act done to the act authorized;
- (h) whether or not the instrumentality by which the harm is done had been furnished by the master to the servant;
- (i) the extent of departure from the normal method of accomplishing an authorized result; and
- (j) whether or not the act is seriously criminal.

APPENDIX D

Florida Statute Section 509.201(1)

'509.201 Room rates; posting; advertising; penalties. —

(1) In each public lodging establishment renting by the day or week there shall be posted in a plainly legible fashion, in a conspicuous place in each rental unit, the rates at which each such unit is rented. Such posting shall show the maximum amount charged for occupancy per person; the amount charged for extra conveniences, more complete accommodations, or additional furnishings; and the dates during the year when such charges prevail. Copies of the posted rate schedules for all similar rental units in each establishment shall be filed with the division at least 5 days before such rates are to become effective and shall be kept current. The rates posted in the rental units shall coincide with those on file in the division's office, and no establishment shall charge more than the rates posted in the rental units and filed with the division.

CASE INDEX

A

Anderson v. Covert, 64
Arnaud's Restaurant, Inc. v. Cotten, 52, 58

B

Black v. Heininger, 71
Brien v. 18925 Collins Avenue Corp., 84
Buck v. Hankin, 35, 36, 38

C

Cedar Rapids Inv. Co. v. Commodore Hotel Co., 7
City of Independence v. Richardson, 8
Cliett v. Lauderdale Biltmore Corporation, 49
Coath v. Jones, 83
Columbia By The Sea, Inc. v. Petty, 63
Conklin v. Hotel Waldorf Astoria Corp., 59
Crawford v. Pacific States Sav. & Loan Co., 89
Cromwell v. Stephens, 8

D

Danile v. Oak Park Arms Hotel, Inc., 68
deSaric v. Miami Caribe Investments, Inc., 43
Dold v. Outrigger Hotel, 96

E

Easley v. Apollo Detective Agency, 84

F

Federal Ins. Co. v. Waldorf Astoria Hotel, 46
Flagiello v. Pennsylvania Hospital, 18
Flax v. Monticello, 98
Fruehauf Corporation v. Aetna Ins. Co., 85

G

Gardyjan v. Tatone, 48
Gary Hotel Courts Inc. v. Perry, 93
Golden v. Lipkind, 87
Goldman v. Hollywood Beach Hotel Co., 89
Gordon v. Hotel Seville Inc., 94
Great American Insurance Co. v. Coppedge, 99

H

Hanover Insurance Co. v. Alamo Motel, 34
Harold Corporation v. Herzberg, 90
Harvey v. DeWeil, 67
Heart of Atlanta Motel Inc. v. U.S., 11
Highlands Ins. Co. v. Gilday, 72
Hillinghorst v. Heart of Atlanta Motel, Inc., 91
Hillman Hotel, Inc. v. McHaley, 88
Hinman v. Westinghouse Electric Co., 61
Howth v. Franklin, 6

J

Jackson v. Steinberg, 99
Jax Liquors, Inc. v. Hall, 85
Johnston v. Mobile Hotel Co., 36, 43

K

Kalpakian v. Oklahoma Sheraton Corporation, 39
Kimple v. Foster, 79

L

Lackman v. Department of Labor and Industries, 33
Lane v. Cotten, 6
Ledington v. Williams, 64
Lynch v. Hotel Bond Co., 49

M

Marbury v. Madison, 18
Milner Hotels v. Brent, 97

Mitchell v. Resto, 60
Mitchell v. The Shoals, Inc., 59
Moritz v. Pines Hotel, Inc., 66

N

Newton v. Candace, Inc., 65
Newell v. Zurich Insurance Co., 89
Nixon v. Royal Coach Inn of Houston, 71, 74

P

Palagano v. Georgian Terrace Hotel Co., 92
Perminas v. Montgomery Ward Co., 29
Peters v. Holiday Inns, Inc., 76
Phillips Petroleum Co. v. Dorn, 73
Poulos v. Brady, 70

R

Reibolt v. Bedient, 59, 80
Reilly v. 180 Club Inc., 80
Rosier v. Gainesville Inns Assoc. Ltd., 73, 74

S

Schermer v. Fremar Corp., 10
Skyways Motor Lodge v. General Foods Corp., 38, 39
Stark v. Chock Full O' Nuts, 58

W

Walkoviak v. Hilton, 75
Wallinga v. Johnson, 37
Waugh v. Duke, 90
Webster v. Blue Ship Tea Room, Inc., 54

Z

Zacharia v. Harbor Island Spa, Inc., 45
Zurich Fire Ins. Co. of New York v. Weil, 35

SUBJECT INDEX

A
Absolute liability, 28
Accommodation, duty of, 5, 6, 11
Assaults by employees, 66
Assumption of risk, 31

B
Bathtub, injuries, 91

C
Case law, 17
Chair, injury, 92, 93
Comparative negligence, 31
Constitution, Federal, 14
Contributory negligence, 31
Court systems, 19, 20

D
Damages, punitive, 27
Discrimination, 11
Dogs, 69, 70
Doors, sliding glass, 90

E
Employees
  assaults by, 66
  selection of, 68
  scope of employment, 69
Employment, scope of, 62

F
Food service
  'foreign' substance in, 53
  furnishing of as 'sale', 49
  implied warranty, 48
  'natural' substance in, 54, 57
  under U.C.C., 52, 53
Found property, 97
Furniture, injuries, 92, 93

G
Glass door, sliding, 90
Guest, injury by other guest, 78, 80
Guest property, liability of innkeeper for
  common law liability, 34
  exceptions, 35
  public enemy, act of, 36
  robbers, 36
  statutory liability, 38

H
History, hotel, motel, 5, 8, 10
House detectives, 64

I
Innkeeper, status as, 6, 7
  duty to accommodate, 5, 6, 11
  insurer, generally not, 88

J
Jurisdiction, 19
  appellate
  original

L
Last clear chance, 31
Locks, doors, 73, 74

M
Maintenance of premises, general, 87

N
Negligence, 28

P
Plaintiff, 20

R
Recreational facilities, 93, 94
Reservations, 96
Respondeat superior, 60, 61
Room assignment, liability for, 75

S
Scope of employment, 62, 69
Security measures, need for, 72, 78
Security personnel
 independent contractors, 84, 85
 prior record, 83
 use of force by, 82
Slip and fall
 general, 87
 hotel driveway, 89
 notice of hazard, 88
 walkways, 89
Stare decisis, 18
Statutes, 14
Summons, 20
Swimming pools, 93, 94

T
Tort, 27

V
Vicarious liability, 60, 63